BOOKS BY ROBERT NORWOOD

HIS GLORIOUS BODY

THE MAN WHO DARED TO BE GOD

THE STEEP ASCENT

THE HERESY OF ANTIOCH

MOTHER AND SON

HIS LADY OF THE SONNETS

THE WITCH OF ENDOR

THE PIPER AND THE REED

THE MODERNISTS

THE MAN OF KERIOTH

BILL BORAM

HIS GLORIOUS BODY

BY
ROBERT NORWOOD
RECTOR OF ST. BARTHOLOMEW'S CHURCH IN THE
CITY OF NEW YORK

*That it may be fashioned like unto his
glorious body.*—PHILIPPIANS III: 21.

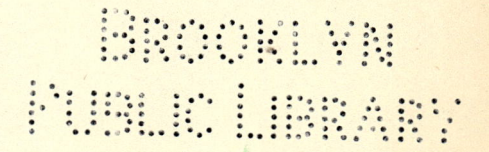

CHARLES SCRIBNER'S SONS
NEW YORK · LONDON
1930

COPYRIGHT, 1930, BY
CHARLES SCRIBNER'S SONS

Printed in the United States of America

TO
MY FATHER
WHO HANDED ME HIS TORCH

FOREWORD

In response to many requests, I offer this companion to "The Steep Ascent," hoping that the Lenten noontide meditations for this year will be as kindly received as its predecessor.

It is not easy to think one's way through the maze of theological thought or to make clear to others what one believes to be the truth concerning the most astounding event in the history of man on this planet. That history is not confined to earth. Man is more than a body; he is a soul. Science has proved what the Bible long ago declared, that man's body is derived from the dust of the ground. But it is not able to prove that this body is animated by a living soul, bearing the image and likeness of God. Such proof transcends the scope of scientific thought. It belongs to the experience of the communion of saints. The natural man—the physical man—derived from the dust of the ground, can only account for himself, as Paul stated. The spiritual man—man a soul, son of

FOREWORD

the living God—must account for himself by obedience to those tests which the Father has ordained for us all and which Jesus of Nazareth, our Lord and Master, proved in his life.

These meditations are based mainly on the accepted letters of the apostle Paul. If one had only the first letter to the Christians at Corinth, one would have sufficient data to justify a full-orbed belief in the historical fact of the death and Resurrection of Jesus. This fact is the amazing event on which these meditations were given this year at St. Bartholomew's, and they represent conclusions which I have reached after much thought.

There was a time when I stopped at the cross, content with the glorious surrender of him who said, "I, when I am lifted up from the earth, will draw all men to myself." Perplexed by the Higher Critics, who had reduced for me the four Gospels to a mosaic of many artists covering the faith of the first and second centuries, and constrained by their arguments at least to accept the apparent contradictions of those writings, I filtered away a gnat to swallow a camel. But the experience of the years forced

FOREWORD

me at last to kneel in humility before those Gospels. Their contradictions, which were superficial, deepened the truth concerning the cross and the open tomb. The written form in which those narratives were set was inspired by an information of something so rarely new that no literary genius could possibly describe it.

Then it was that one day I read carefully the first letter to the Corinthians. This letter, written twenty-five years after the crucifixion and long before the Evangelists had told their story, carried its own authority. Paul was not converted by the four Gospels. He anticipated them. His letter was written at a time when his great ministry was in its ascendant. He was already known as a convert. His enemies could at any time have challenged the facts which he produced when he wrote to the Corinthians. No one seems openly to have challenged them, though he was often in debate with the disciples of the first century about certain details which his peculiar method of administration involved.

According to the letter to the Galatians, Paul, some time after his conversion, spent a

FOREWORD

fortnight with Simon Peter in Jerusalem. What was the subject of their conversation? Jesus. Simon would confirm Paul's experience of the Resurrection with his own story; that story is found in the Marcan Gospel. Surely these two men were not deceived. Christ did die for our sins and rose again the third day according to the scriptures.

Two facts are before us. These facts are basic to Christianity and without them it has no historical foundation. I dwell upon them in these meditations because their validity has been challenged through the centuries and with an increasing vehemence to-day. Why? Because the world of physical and mental consciousness does not easily surrender to the witness of Jesus that man is a living soul. Human pride shrinks from submission to the spiritual supremacy of any one, however good. Something in us tears at and tries to drag down whatever surpasses human averages. We are suspicious of excellence. Having been deceived by appearance, we often cover with cynicism the wounds which the occasional thrust of disappointment has made in our hearts. The religion offered us in

FOREWORD

our childhood has not squared with the facts of experience. Like Jesus, some of us have lamented, "Ye have made it a den of thieves," and have turned from the temple, embittered against religion. Life is indeed a disenchanting process. As we grow older, our hopes fade, our enthusiasms cool, our laughter dwindles, until our love of the ideal languishes behind the imprisoning bars of disappointment, frustration, and despair. We recoil from repeating those emotions which used to kindle at the thought of the fulfilment of our purest impulses. We are like the disciples on the road to Emmaus. With them we debate and argue, refusing to accept the old challenge which once we so gladly obeyed.

Having passed through a sorrow too deep for words, we are afraid to expose ourselves to its renewed shock by setting free the imprisoned splendor of our early faith in the goodness of life. Life cannot be good if death frustrates love. The cold green sea breaks upon the gray stones of a loveless shore. If death ends life, it also ends love; for how can love continue when life is engulfed in the oblivion of death?

This describes the experience of the first dis-

FOREWORD

ciples; and the Emmaus walk leads through every human heart. A dead body is a sacred thing, and when the grave has taken it forever away from loving eyes, wistful lips, searching hands, the heart can stand no more, not even the hope that it might again beat with that other heart now crumbling in the tomb. There is an austere nobility in this state of mind that shrinks from exposing the sanctity of a body so loved to those who stamp upon the grave with indifferent feet. Our tears have been sealed in a bottle. Can we submit that fragile jar to careless fingers? No! Hide it away; it contains the wine of a broken heart.

Paul went through this experience, and possibly that is the reason why, according to his own confession, he felt that he ought to do many things contrary to the name of Jesus Christ of Nazareth.

Into these sentences I have written the story of my own heart, and in what follows I have tried to tell something of that joy which my heart knew when at last, like Paul, I ceased to kick against the pricks and surrendered to the fact of the Resurrection.

[xiv]

FOREWORD

Companions of the path which Jesus walked for us all, there is no death! What we call death is an adventure through which our souls are strengthened as we pass unfalteringly on the way to the knowledge of eternal life. Jesus died to prove that there is nothing in death for us to fear. Jesus saw man as he will one day be when God is all in all. He believed in himself as a son of God. He also believed in us as brothers, sons of that Infinite Father. By the downward point of his cross, he pierced the dread of death, as by its upward and outward points, he surveyed and titled our claim to the heritage of eternal life.

ROBERT NORWOOD.

St. Bartholomew's Church,
  New York,
    November 22, 1929.

ACKNOWLEDGMENT

The author gratefully acknowledges the courtesy of Mr. George H. Doran for permission to use quotations from Dr. Moffatt's translation of the Old and New Testaments.

CONTENTS

CHAPTER		PAGE
I.	First and Foremost	3
II.	A New Day	15
III.	The Communion of Saints	24
IV.	Hermon and Bethany	35
V.	Our Potential Godhood	45
VI.	God's Secret Purpose	52
VII.	Man and His Father	63
VIII.	The Power of the Resurrection	71
IX.	Paul and Peter	80
X.	The New Creation	89
XI.	Our Glorious Body	98
XII.	Spiritual Athletics	108
XIII.	The Fulness of God	118
XIV.	Clothed with Immortality	128
XV.	One Body and One Spirit	136
XVI.	The Glory of Man's Inheritance	147

CONTENTS

CHAPTER		PAGE
XVII.	THE WITNESS OF WORDS	158
XVIII.	THE CHURCH OF GOD	170
XIX.	STARS IN A DARK WORLD	182
XX.	VISIBLE AND INVISIBLE WORLDS	193
XXI.	GOD'S ARMOR	204
XXII.	OUR BELOVED BROTHER	219

HIS GLORIOUS BODY

I

FIRST AND FOREMOST

I Corinthians xv : 1–11

"Now, brothers, I would have you know the gospel I once preached to you, the gospel you received, the gospel in which you have your footing, the gospel by which you are saved—provided you adhere to my statement of it—unless indeed your faith was all haphazard.

"First and foremost, I passed on to you what I had myself received, namely, that Christ died for our sins as the scriptures had said, that he was buried, that he rose on the third day as the scriptures had said, and that he was seen by Cephas, then by the twelve; after that, he was seen by over five hundred brothers all at once, the majority of whom survive to this day, though some have died; after that, he was seen by James, then by all the apostles, and finally he was seen by myself, by this so-called 'abortion' of an apostle. For I am the very least of the apostles, unfit to bear the name of apostle,

since I persecuted the church of God. But by God's grace I am what I am. The grace he showed me did not go for nothing; no, I have done far more work than all of them—though it was not I but God's grace at my side. At any rate, whether I or they have done most, such is what we preach, such is what you believed."

CHRISTIANITY began with a cross and an open tomb. But the cross and the tomb could have had no meaning without the life preceding them. It is the Man on the cross and in the tomb who gives to both the profound spiritual meaning of Christianity. The life of a hero is a test of our highest and best; and when the hero gathers in himself all that we hope and dream and will for the best that is in ourselves, he lives forever in our hearts.

To discover the reason why Jesus died is to gain the secret of his power over men through all these years. Once we have made that secret ours, it becomes the transforming and renewing principle of our lives.

As we study the message of the New Testament, we find that it rests upon the dual facts

FIRST AND FOREMOST

of the death and the Resurrection of Jesus. Though there still are people who doubt its historical truth, the fact of the cross is now well established. But the open tomb has not the same evidence. The cross appeals to us because it measures the fineness of Jesus' soul. We all know a cross and understand something about it. But the victory of the tomb is another matter. It is easy to accept the victory of a cross; it is not so easy to accept the victory of a tomb.

But we must not mutilate the message of the New Testament. We must take it in its entirety or not at all. Can we submit to the appeal of the nobility of the Master's life, placing the laurels of our adoration at the foot of his cross, and withholding those same tributes from the door of an open tomb? If the life of Jesus has won us to a better way of living, his death must also demand of us a better way of dying. It is not enough for a follower of the Master to adore him for the beauty of his character and thank God that at least one man proved our human merit. We must let that life possess us completely and lift us beyond all doubts concerning our survival after death. If Jesus means anything at all to us, he is more than a challenge to noble living; he is also a challenge to our serenity in the presence of death. Many of us have no serenity before a tomb. We have vague hopes that somehow we shall go beyond it, but those hopes are not the stalwart faith which strengthened the disciples of the first century.

Modern thought is trying to prove the survival of the soul by divers methods. These methods are commendable wherever they represent our hunger for God and eternal life with Him. But the one supreme evidence which ought to set our doubts forever at rest is disregarded as though it were historically unreliable.

Let us approach this matter with an open mind, with tolerance, reverence, and tenderness. We must not seem to strike at any prop which supports a lonely and grief-stricken comrade. Surely we are the richer for these methods of modern thought, and surely it is in harmony with the spirit of the Master to go on all roads that end at Emmaus. If by psychical research any scientific demonstration of human survival after death is found, one has only gratitude to offer those who are honest students of psychic phenomena. We have no right to close our minds against any comrade upon his road of adventure toward the Promised Land. We have our own experiences—many of them beautiful and satisfying—but they are so vague and illusive that we hesitate to offer them to others. These experiences are like manna which, though gathered for the day to sustain the Israelites upon their march through the wilderness, could not be gathered up and contained in even the most fragile jar.

The psychologists are disquieting. They seem to have removed many of our foundations. Not that they have been altogether successful, but none the less no thoughtful person can utterly disregard many of the astounding and discomforting conclusions of psychology. We all know that our bodies and souls are strangely commingled; that it is difficult to distinguish between our physical, mental, and spiritual states. The body has much to do with the mind and the soul. When the body is tired, it is exposed to temptation from without and from within. If the body is healthy, we have open vision and clear understanding. But when it is overstrained by the pressure of life, what a brooding and almost incurable melancholy seizes us! The psychologists use this knowledge to the uttermost, so that what was regarded as good evidence in the first century has little, if any, value to-day. Yet it is our duty to follow through all trails that lead to information concerning the soul.

Theosophy offers information, though, like psychology, it is based on an intellectual *ipse dixit* whose hypotheses are not always provable. There may be *mahatmas*, supermen at work on this planet, but one has to take the word of a Blavatsky or a Sinnett or a Besant. But shall we sneer at books like "The Secret Doctrine"? As well sneer at Commander Byrd. We have heard people say: "Why should this explorer undertake such arduous and profitless adventures?" As though man has not always been furthered by the adventurous spirit of those who blaze lonely trails! Occasionally these adventurers return with information which changes the whole course of human thought and action, even when that information rests mainly upon the integrity of the explorer.

If we accept the teaching of Christian Science, we must look on death as an illusion. Many people have been comforted by so regarding death. But was death an illusion to Jesus? And is it an illusion to us?

Our bodies are not illusory. If they are, then the soul is only an idea. There is such a thing as physical death—the break-up of the body—and it is that disintegration of our physical selfhood with which we are concerned when we speak of death. The body that was crucified and taken down from the cross to be laid in a sepulchre was not an illusion. It was an eternal fact. If not, the Incarnation can have no appeal, no meaning. He who said, "Feel me and see; a ghost has not flesh and bones as you see I have," asserted the historical, the spatial, character of his body. While there is much that is beautiful and true in Christian Science, our way through an open tomb is not to be found by calling it an error of the mind.

The psychologist rests his case on the fact of the body. He is honestly trying to understand it and account for its moods as well as for its relation with other bodies. He can only lift his eyebrows in amazement at those who assert the illusory character of our mortal habitation, basing upon that their belief in immortality.

It is evident, from this brief survey of modern methods, that the survival of the soul cannot be demonstrated by reason. It is here that the testimony of the first century makes its appeal to the followers of Jesus. We are trying to find our way back through the centuries to the Galilean Carpenter. We rest our case for immortality upon him, and him alone. He came into the world nineteen hundred years ago, lived a short but wonderful life which satisfied his friends that through him God had come at last to men. That life was ended by a crucifixion.

Up to the point of his crucifixion, the disciples of Jesus never thought that he could be killed on a cross. When they found that their Master was dead, they were broken, amazed, and lost in the most terrible despair that has ever engulfed the faith of humanity. The first and awful fact about the beginning of Christianity is that Jesus, on whom the hopes of his disciples rested, was defeated by the death of his body on a cross.

There are clever people who argue that the

FIRST AND FOREMOST

story of the Resurrection grew out of the need of the disciples to recover their faith in the Master; that the experience through which they passed when they saw him dead was so shattering that it exposed them to a series of illusions, out of which grew the gospel of the Resurrection. The stern facts of the New Testament are irresistible and render this explanation absurd. The witnesses are unanimous, and their evidence holds together. They were overthrown by the death of Jesus. They had no anticipation of his Resurrection, for they had no means of reaching beyond the disaster of Golgotha. Their Master could not die! He might go so far as the cross, but in a moment his Christhood would be demonstrated by a terrible punishment falling from heaven upon those who dared to touch his sacred body. How they waited, even when they saw their Master's eyes glaze in death, for the manifestation of his power; and when that thorn-crowned head drooped wearily at last, they ran away terrified—not because they were afraid of their Master's enemies but because their faith in him as the Messiah was completely destroyed.

To say that such a mood of despair could be

recovered by a series of illusions is to ask of our human nature something which it has never revealed. Frustrated idealists do not within a little while recover from such a disaster to become the leaders of a new movement in the quest of God through the survival of the soul over the death of the body which it has incarnated.

The first Epistle to the Corinthians is accepted by the critics as a composition of the apostle Paul—as one of the earliest historical records within twenty-five years of the crucifixion. This epistle was written some time after Paul had visited the city of Corinth, where he had established a church or community grouped about the two cardinal facts of the gospel. It must be remembered that the four documents attributed to Matthew, Mark, Luke, and John had not yet been written; also that the story told by the four Evangelists had been opposed by Paul up to the time of his conversion.

Thus far we are on solid ground. Whatever this letter contains witnesses to the nature of the preaching current from the earliest activity of the original disciples to the moment when Paul addressed himself to the Corinthians.

FIRST AND FOREMOST

"First and foremost," he states, "I passed on to you what I had myself received, namely, that Christ died for our sins as the scriptures had said, that he rose on the third day as the scriptures had said."

What scriptures? It is evident that the apostle meant, first, a fulfilment of Old Testament prophecy; and second, the historical narratives which were beginning to appear preliminary to the four Gospels as we now have them. This shows that the first disciples were able, from a new experience with their Master, to realize that the great moments of the Old Testament moved up gradually to the supreme moment of the New—the death and the Resurrection of Jesus. Of this Paul was convinced. His conversion turned upon that conviction. His preaching was constantly renewed and inspired by it. The cross and the open tomb had become for Paul the two pillars of the Christian faith.

PRAYER

Be with us in our approach to Thee, loving Father. Grant that we may so direct our thought that we may come into Thy presence purified by sincerity from every stain of sin. We acknowledge our fault, and our sin is ever before us. Crooked and devious are the trails of our minds. We love ourselves more than we love Thee, and sell Thee in the market-place for pieces of silver. Help us to be honest with ourselves, to behold in the mirror of the pure heart of Jesus our faces, that we may detect every dishonest act, every covert deed, every unworthy thought or word. Help us to be lifted so high that we may be quiet above the noise of life.

When in our weary moments we find the insufficiency of our spiritual strength, be present with us and cover us with Thy wings. Give us courage and strength to resist whatever tempts us to break faith with Thee. We do not expect to reach Thee without struggle, for we know our world—its dangers and its perils. But we seek Thee through all these things, and call now upon Thee for grace to follow the Master to the end of the road. Amen.

II

A NEW DAY

I Corinthians xv : 12–20

"Now if we preach that Christ rose from the dead, how can certain individuals among you assert that 'there is no such thing as a resurrection of the dead'? If 'there is no such thing as a resurrection from the dead,' then even Christ did not rise; and if Christ did not rise, then our preaching has gone for nothing, and your faith has gone for nothing too. Besides, we are detected bearing false witness to God by affirming of him that he raised Christ —whom he did not raise, if after all dead men never rise. For if dead men never rise, Christ did not rise either; and if Christ did not rise, your faith is futile, you are still in your sins. More than that: those who have slept the sleep of death in Christ have perished after all. Ah, if in this life we have nothing but a mere hope in Christ, we are of all men to be pitied most!

"But it is not so! Christ did rise from the

dead, he was the first to be reaped of those who sleep in death."

How are we to take these words? Are they the words of a knave, or a fool, or a saint? Each of us must answer that question according to his understanding and experience. We know that every work of art is its own defense. However much critics may disagree among themselves, truth and beauty are justified by their spirit. So we reach our conclusions concerning everything that is challenged: Is it true? Is it beautiful? If we can answer those questions in the affirmative, we may go hand in hand down the years with every experience which truth and beauty ensoul.

That is how we must feel when we approach the witness of Paul to the fact of the Resurrection. Against the attacks of a concerted unbelief, these words are vital and real. They do not sound like the words of a knave or of a fool. They are the words of a good man. He may have been deceived, and he may have been mixed in his thinking. But the quality of truth and sincerity is too evident to justify our casual handling of the astounding statement that a man who died on a cross came back again to many people, and finally to Paul himself, in such a way as to change the lives of those who shared this new experience, making them intrepid gospellers of immortal life.

What we need at this moment is to scrutinize, not the statement, but the mood of men concerning the soul's adventure into the infinite. It has been said that people do not care to go on; that they are more interested in life now than in life hereafter. Doubtless some men and women have no interest in life beyond this planet, but one has only to look backward over life to the gray dawn of civilization to discover that the thought of immortality has stirred humanity to its noblest deeds.

Even our doubts on this matter are important, since they make us one with all the pioneers of the upward path. Paul himself at one time shared these doubts. That is why he persecuted the followers of Jesus. Their statement that Jesus had survived death seemed to him not only absurd but blasphemous. If the thing were true, then all previous experience with life would have to be restated, because it placed Jesus in a unique relationship with God. This appears in a fugitive utterance of Paul:

> "Jews demand miracles and Greeks want wisdom, but our message is Christ the crucified—a stumbling-block to the Jews, 'sheer folly' to the Gentiles, but for those who are called, whether Jews or Greeks, a Christ who is the power of God and the wisdom of God."

How like the original witnesses is Paul in his doubting mood! Read Luke's account of the walk to Emmaus:

> "That very day two of them were on their way to a village called Emmaus about seven miles from Jerusalem. They were conversing about all these events, and during their conversation and discussion Jesus himself approached and walked beside them, though they were prevented from recognizing him. He said to them, 'What is all this you are debating on your walk?' They stopped, looking downcast, and one of them, called Cleopas, answered him, 'Are you a lone stranger in Jerusalem, not to know what has been happening there?' 'What is that?' he said to them. They replied, 'All about Jesus of Nazaret! To God and all the people he was a prophet strong in action and utterance, but the high priests and our rulers delivered him up to be sentenced to death and crucified him. Our own hope was that he would be the redeemer of Israel; but he is dead, and that is three days ago! Though some women of our number

gave us a surprise; they were at the tomb early in the morning and could not find his body, but they came to tell us they had actually seen a vision of angels who declared he was alive. Some of our company did go to the tomb and found things exactly as the women had said, but they did not see him.' He said to them, 'O foolish men, with hearts so slow to believe, after all the prophets have declared!'"

There we have the old, old difficulty of the spiritual overcoming the mortal mind; the old, old difficulty of assuming our heavenly citizenship. The difficulty is easily explained if we believe that man was incarnated for the enrichment and unfolding of his spiritual self; that this planet is a school of many grades, to which he comes to learn the elements of divine knowledge. God is making man in His image and after His likeness.

We know too much about our mortal manhood to make the mistake of identifying it with God. Death, sickness, and sin live in that manhood. But deep within this visible man there lives the invisible, or spiritual, man. Paul described him: "Strengthened by his Spirit in the inner man. . . . The Spirit itself testifying along with our own spirit that we are children of God."

Have we any information of this spiritual man? Yes. The saints are such witnesses; there have been, and there are, men and women who have revealed a power that transcends all physical and mental experience. We, too, have our occasional ascents to immortal mind. Our enthusiasm for any kind of beauty or truth is a faint expression of its reality. Are we to stop at the things which are seen? Must we limit ourselves to those states of consciousness which touch us as we eat, and drink, and work, and play, and rest? Paul answers: "No, for the seen is transient, the unseen eternal." We are only on the borderland of consciousness, and we must not shut our eyes to the glory that already shines on the faces of those who have gone a little way ahead of us.

Much has been said to stress the obvious contradictions of the Evangelists. But are those contradictions fundamental? Do they not rather give reality to the story of the open tomb? Are they not what one would expect from men and women entering into a startling and unexpected experience?

Our difficulty is not so much in accepting the

story of the Resurrection, as in surrendering to its implications. If Jesus came back, who is he? How are we related to him? Every hero is a mediator between old and new adventures. Every genius is a trumpeter, calling us out of sleep. We are not easily awakened, and we complain at the discomforts of early rising. It is pleasant to drowse and sleep, and wake and drowse again. But we cannot always disregard an early morning summons. We must rise up and face the day, and go about our tasks. So Paul wrote to the Corinthians: "Watch, stand firm in the faith, play the man, be strong!"

The gospel of the Resurrection is an early morning summons to a new day. We must meet that day with a new mind, the mind of complete surrender to the Man who has called us out of darkness into light. Paul was summoned, and he obeyed. When he discovered that Jesus had overcome death, his gratitude was so boundless that he said: "God forbid that I should glory in anything but him. I count everything lost that I may win Christ."

Wherever men have surrendered to the resurrected Jesus, they have always had his resur-

HIS GLORIOUS BODY

rection power; for we are all involved in the cross. We have all touched death. But why should we stop there? In touching the death of our loved ones, we have touched the death of Jesus. Why not carry the Resurrection of Jesus into the resurrection of our loved ones? By every oath of God, by all the wonder and the beauty of the soul of Jesus, there are no dead!

If that is true; if there stands among us One who has passed through the terror of dying to bring back to us the assurance of immortality, what can we do but give ourselves fully to him? Our difficulty is not an intellectual but a moral one. Our question is not so much: Is it true? but, Am I true to it?

PRAYER

Breathe on us, Breath of God, that we may know that we are His children, heirs of His nature, and destined to share His fulness bodily.

Breathe on us, Breath of God, that we may set our sonship against the perils of the sea and of the land, of the cold and of the heat, of the drought and of the rain, of our countrymen, of our intimate friends, of strangers who try to rob us of that sonship—perils of this hardened world, the world that is too much with us, overlaying us with its weight of matter.

Breathe on us that we may resurrect into our eternal consciousness, rising above the illusion of death, knowing that the things that were written, were written that we may know that now we have eternal life, revealed in him whom we adore, Jesus the Christ and Saviour of the world. Amen.

III

THE COMMUNION OF SAINTS

I Corinthians xv : 35–42

"But, someone will ask, 'how do the dead rise? What kind of body have they when they come?' Foolish man! What you sow never comes to life unless it dies. And what you sow is not the body that is to be; it is a mere grain of wheat, for example, or some other seed. God gives it a body as he pleases, gives each kind of seed a body of its own. Flesh is not all the same; there is human flesh, there is flesh of beasts, flesh of birds, and flesh of fish. There are heavenly bodies and also earthly bodies, but the splendour of the heavenly body is one thing and the splendour of the earthly is another. There is a splendour of the sun and a splendour of the moon and a splendour of the stars—for one star differs from another in splendour. So with the resurrection of the dead."

MANY sincere thinkers set aside this portion of the Corinthian letter, and not a few of Paul's

THE COMMUNION OF SAINTS

most ardent lovers regret that it was written. "Impossible, antiquated, and altogether unworthy of his genius," they say.

Our trouble is that we still see through a glass, darkly, the events with which the argument of Paul is concerned. The important fact is that the letter comes to us with the authority of the man who wrote it. Paul had met the living Jesus. If he did not meet him, then we must regard one of the holiest and sanest of men as a liar or a fool.

Some have said that the writer had a sunstroke on the way to Damascus, and that the experience on which this letter is based originated in an hallucination. But men with sunstrokes do not write with the clarity and conviction which we find in the Corinthian letter. Hallucinations do not belong to the character of the man whose story is told in the Acts of the Apostles.

We have the alternative of calling this man a liar. It is the only way out. But he was too intellectually and spiritually consistent to be a liar or the victim of an hallucination. The Resurrection of Jesus stands upon one of the surest foundations of human evidence.

HIS GLORIOUS BODY

We have already examined some of the reasons why people find it hard to believe that Paul met the risen Jesus. Some do not believe for the very joy of it—too good to be true!—and some shrink from it because of the awful challenge in the story of the resurrected Jesus. It is a challenge to a changed life, a challenge which few of us are prepared to accept.

If Jesus lives, all who have gone before us are alive. They sleep as to their bodies, but they live as to their souls. They are more alive now than they were when they had physical bodies. Death has released them from the old to a new body, with new powers of vision, hearing, and understanding. How clearly they see the consequences of their life in the flesh, and how fully aware they are of those whom they have left behind! They now know why they were with us and why they have left us.

"Therefore, with all this host of witnesses encircling us, we must strip off every handicap, strip off sin with its clinging folds, to run our appointed course steadily, our eyes fixed upon Jesus as the pioneer and the perfection of faith—upon Jesus who, in order to reach his own appointed joy, steadily endured the cross, thinking nothing of its shame, and is now seated at the right hand of the throne of God.

THE COMMUNION OF SAINTS

Compare him who steadily endured all that hostility from sinful men, so as to keep your own hearts from fainting and failing."

Of course, this passage does not establish the communion of saints. But there is an implication here that seems to whisper from a higher life: "Be on your guard. We are watching you. We love you. We know your trials, for we have passed through them."

A young poet said in a recent conversation: "Poetry comes through by austerity, mental struggle, and courage. It is a flame from a fine jet. There is no other art that calls for such full surrender of the will, the intelligence, and the emotions as the art of poetry." But the painter, the musician, the sculptor, would also say this for his art. It is always true that beauty makes this demand of its ministers: "Thou shalt have no other gods before me."

Think of the reaction of a man like Paul to the challenge of the risen Lord. He was too alert, too quick in his thinking, not to see that this experience with a new form of human life demanded of him an unconditional surrender to Jesus:

"Well then, my brothers, I appeal to you by all the mercy of God to dedicate your bodies as a living sacrifice, consecrated and acceptable to God; that is your cult, a spiritual rite. Instead of being moulded to this world, have your mind renewed, and so be transformed in nature, able to make out what the will of God is, namely, what is good and acceptable to him and perfect. . . .

"Let your love be a real thing, with loathing for evil and a bent for what is good. Put affection into your love for the brotherhood; be forward to honour one another; never let your zeal flag; maintain the spiritual glow; serve the Lord; let your hope be a joy in you; be stedfast in trouble, attend to prayer, contribute to needy saints, make a practice of hospitality. Bless those who make a practice of persecuting you; bless them instead of cursing them. Rejoice with those who rejoice, and weep with those who weep. Keep in harmony with one another; instead of being ambitious, associate with humble folk; never be self-conceited. Never pay back evil for evil to anyone; aim to be above reproach in the eyes of all; be at peace with all men, if possible, so far as that depends on you."

These were some of Paul's conscious reactions to the challenge of the risen Jesus. He could not go on living according to the former man. The experience with the Master made inevitable a new relationship with the world. No one in fairness can read these words without measuring this new standard of life. Could one enter into such an experience and go on living as before? Impossible! As the artist approaches beauty, in humility and with a new mind, so must we surrender to Paul if we would follow him into Damascus.

While we have been thinking of these things, one question has disturbed us: If our beloved are aware of us from the plane of a new understanding, how can they be at peace? Let the author of the Revelation of St. John reply:

"And when he opened the fifth seal, I saw underneath the altar the souls of those who had been slain for adhering to God's word and to the testimony which they bore; and they cried aloud, 'O Sovereign Lord, holy and true, how long wilt thou refrain from charging and avenging our blood upon those who dwell on earth?' But they were each given a white robe, and told to remain quiet for a little longer, until their number was completed by their fellow-servants and their brothers who were to be killed like themselves."

This description of the concern of our departed comrades justifies our conclusion that death has not separated us from them. They are one with us, though they have a larger view of the plan of God. As a man looks back in sympathy upon his younger brother struggling up through the grades of the old school from which he long ago graduated, so do they whom death has released, regard us. Is it too much to say of them that their perfection depends as much upon us, as ours depends upon them? Said the Master: "I am the vine; ye are the branches," claiming to be one with us in a brotherhood of divine sons who, as they go from glory to glory, look back to help and encourage those who follow after them.

All this makes the unpopular section of Paul's argument for immortality one of his most important utterances. The fact of the risen Jesus establishes the fact of the risen life for all men. And it does more than this: it describes the nature of that new life. We are not to think that the soul is provided with a new body the moment death has destroyed the old, for there is a natural body and there is a spiritual body. They exist together. We have them now. Death is only a discarding of that exterior flesh body, so admirably adjusted to our present material environment. We no longer need that body when we pass into the blessed state

THE COMMUNION OF SAINTS

of the departed. We go on with the spiritual body which we have now, though it is not manifested as it will be after death destroys the physical body.

This touches upon the ethical system of Paul. Having discovered the inner body of man through the risen Jesus, he set out to develop that same body in himself. Sin, according to his thought, was disastrous because it denied the reality of the spiritual body. To the Christians in Corinth and elsewhere he said in substance: "If you would share with our Master the body of the inner man which he revealed to me on the road to Damascus, even as he revealed it to Peter and his brethren, you must begin consciously to occupy it before death comes. Do not live as though you had only a physical body. If you do, when death comes you will be born into the next phase of life as a malformed and hideous child is born into this life. Do you ask, How do the dead rise and what kind of body have they when they come? Foolish man! Can you not see that they rise with the body which they have even now? But that body will not be able to function on the higher plane to which we pass

[31]

when the lower body dies unless we begin now to prepare it. Sow your thought into the reality of the spiritual body. Change your consciousness from a physical to a spiritual body. You have both these bodies. Why dwell in the lower body when you have the higher body? That which is born of the flesh is flesh, and that which is born of the spirit is spirit. The flesh body dies. The spirit body never dies. So be buried with Christ in the death of his physical body that you may be resurrected with him in the deathlessness of his spiritual body. Be not deceived. God is not mocked. If you sow to the flesh body, you will reap the inevitable death to which that body is heir. But if you sow to your spiritual body, you will reap the everlasting life to which it is heir. The Master has come to claim your life in the spirit. Be therefore risen with him that you may live where he now lives, at the right hand of God."

So the resurrection truth confronts us, who know that thought affects the physical body, which resembles, therefore, the manner of our life. A hero looks out of hero's eyes. Tenderness is always on a mother's mouth. The scholar has stamped his life of thought upon his serious and brooding face. By that same law we build statelier mansions for the deathless soul.

PRAYER

O God, who hast made man to be immortal and in whom we live and move and have our being, help us this day that we may lay hold on eternal life. May we enter that life by the power of the cross and the open tomb of our Master; for this is eternal life, to know Thee the only God and Jesus Christ whom Thou hast sent. May we know Thee by touching and claiming him.

There are walls across our road, builded of the bricks of the tower of the confusion of tongues. Help us to destroy these walls. We are weak, though our weakness is made strong by the grace of him who died to help us, and rose again to lead us upon the road which slopes in darkness up to Thee. Help us to cast out sin, that it may no longer reign in our mortal bodies. Examine our hearts in the light of Thy presence. Send out that light and its truth into our innermost being, revealing every

HIS GLORIOUS BODY

corner where sin lurks to raven and destroy. And help us to be loyal to our inheritance of eternal life which we have in Jesus' name. Amen.

IV

HERMON AND BETHANY

I Corinthians xv : 42–55

*"What is sown is mortal,
what rises is immortal;
sown inglorious,
it rises in glory;
sown in weakness,
it rises in power;
sown an animate body,
it rises a spiritual body.*

"As there is an animate body, so there is a spiritual body. Thus it is written:

*'The first man, Adam, became an animate being,
the last Adam a life-giving Spirit;
but the animate, not the spiritual, comes first,
and only then the spiritual.
Man the first is from the earth, material;
Man the second is from heaven.
As Man the material is, so are the material;
as Man the heavenly is, so are the heavenly.
Thus, as we have borne the likeness of material Man,
so we are to bear the likeness of the heavenly Man.'*

"I tell you this, my brothers, flesh and blood cannot inherit the Realm of God, nor can the

perishing inherit the imperishable. Here is a secret truth for you: not all of us are to die, but all of us are to be changed—changed in a moment, in the twinkling of an eye, at the last trumpet-call. The trumpet will sound, the dead will rise imperishable, and we shall be changed. For this perishing body must be invested with the imperishable, and this mortal body invested with immortality; and when this mortal body has been invested with immortality, then the saying of Scripture will be realized,

> *Death is swallowed up in victory.*
> *O Death, where is your victory?*
> *O Death, where is your sting?"*

We inhabit the physical and the spiritual body simultaneously. We do not gain the latter after the breakdown of the former. We have them now, and when the physical body dies, we continue to live in the spiritual body.

All nature seeks embodiment by re-embodiment. This process of re-embodiment is revealed in birth and death. What we call evolution might better be described as re-embodiment. Biology is the science of re-embodiment, new bodies coming out of old bodies. The bodies which we now have die and are born again on an average of every seven years. They have come along the path of birth and death. They are plastic to our thinking. We are a multiple of bodies, whose reality is determined by their centre, the soul.

We are not bodies with souls; we are souls with bodies. Our problem is not involved in the question, Does the soul survive death? but in that other question, Is there survival value in the physical body which the soul now uses? To this we answer, Yes. Biology has traced the slow ascent of life from the amœba to man through re-embodiment. As Paul teaches, the first man is from the earth; the second man is from heaven. As souls we are divine; as physical bodies we are earthy and animal. But what a difference there is between the beginnings of the physical body and the body which the human soul is now using! By the ascent of the life-force through re-embodiment, nature has come at last to a definite expression of divine consciousness through our human organism.

The first man is a physical body. It is described in Genesis as Adam, or earth-man. This body does not resurrect, save by the principle which causes it to persist until the soul has no further need of it. Yet there are elements out of which that body is built which can be transformed by the soul into that other body which the Master revealed after the Resurrection. Even as matter enters into our conscious selfhood by digestion, so gradually is the spiritual body forming within the physical body for the soul's use when it passes through the gate of death to another plane of life.

The Gospel story of the Resurrection must either be denied, accepted, or explained away. According to that story, the body of Jesus was taken down from the cross, wrapped in linen cloths, and placed in a sepulchre, sealed by a stone. On the first day of the week following the burial of Jesus, some of his disciples found the stone rolled away and the sepulchre empty. What happened?

It is said by those who deny the immortality of man that the contradictory details of this story in the four Gospels prove their legendary character. On the other hand, many who believe in Christ's victory over death hesitate to accept the story of the open tomb. It is not our business to debate the matter either with those who deny the fact or with those who accept it with reservations. We are content to rest our case with the historical witness of Paul. If Jesus appeared to him on the road to Damascus, demonstrating the spiritual body of man, then the substantial facts of the Gospel story fall within human experience. Despite the superficial contradictions in that story, Paul is on the side of the open tomb, and if we are to follow his thought through these meditations, we must face this question: What happened after the dead body of Jesus was buried in the sepulchre?

Jesus had already attained deathlessness. He revealed that in the Transfiguration. Why did Jesus on his way down from the mountain seal the lips of Simon, James, and John, telling them to say nothing of what they had seen till such a time as the Son of man rose from the dead? It is our belief that the reason for this secrecy is to be found in the nature of the Transfiguration itself. This event in the life of our Lord marked his victory over death. Later he said to the priests in the temple: "I have power to lay my life down and also power to take it up again." Jesus was aware of that victory and looked with confidence at the cross, believing that by it, and it alone, he could share his Transfiguration with those who accepted him as their Master. By dying on the cross he descended from the height of his Transfiguration to the depth of death itself, and by his Resurrection he regained that height which he now holds for us all.

What happened in the tomb? That which happened on the hill of Transfiguration. The two bodies of Jesus became one body. Death could not destroy that body. He could manifest his divine selfhood under the two aspects of his divine manhood. By obedience to his soul he transubstantiated the physical into the spiritual body; by obedience to the will of God through his surrendered soul he was able, in dying, to separate the lower from the higher body and, in resurrecting, to combine them into that eternal unity of the carnal and the spiritual which lies before us, according to Paul, as the prize of our high calling in God.

HERMON AND BETHANY

Paul believed that as Jesus died, he rose for us all, and wrote his letters to teach us how we, too, might attain that resurrection. The Christian life is an imitation of the life of Jesus. It seeks the transfiguration of the animal body by the interpenetrating splendor of the spiritual body.

However fanciful the story of the open tomb may seem to those who deny the selfhood of God and of the human soul, we who believe that Jesus is the Christ of God rejoice in its certitude. Our hope is not in a dead but in a living Christ. We have no difficulty in accepting the story of the open tomb. Though not a few of our number tear out of the gospel story the page that describes the Transfiguration, we who accept Jesus as the risen Lord walk with the disciples from Hermon to Bethany. On the hill of the Transfiguration, those disciples first saw his glory, as on the hill near Bethany it faded from their eyes when a cloud received him out of sight.

Let us kneel before this risen Christ. He is God's pledge of human survival, who stands in our midst with his word: "Do not be afraid; I am the First and Last, I was dead and here

I am alive for evermore, holding the keys that unlock death and Hades." Our heart aches for the unnumbered thousands of men and women who grope in darkness for the light of immortality. We are not thinking of the selfish and the unloving. Our thought is toward the multitude who are unselfish and loving, whose need for eternity is measured by the agony of bereavement. Has Christianity no consolation for these? Yes; but it cannot be offered with equivocating words.

We have the great simplicities of Paul's letters, with their emphasis upon the facts of the cross and the open tomb. Again we take up his gospel and say to our world as he said to his: "Come, you broken-hearted and you sorrowing. Come with us and walk the old Bethany road; or, if you will, loiter in Mary's garden among the flowers, or along the lake of Galilee, or kneel with us in the upper room where he stands to offer us his hands and his side, saying: 'Behold, it is I and not a phantom.'"

Paul and the Evangelists are in substantial agreement concerning the cross and the sepulchre. The one was as real as the other. As Jesus appeared to the disciples, he appeared to Paul. As they walked with him, so did Paul. As he manifested himself in many ways to Peter, so he did to Paul. Theirs was not a subjective experience nor a vision seen through eyes full of tears. And however glorious was the manifestation of Christ's risen body to Paul on the road to Damascus, it was objective. He heard a voice and he saw a face. They say he was blinded by what he saw, and that was also true of Peter and his brother disciples. They were all blinded, as we are blinded, by the fact of the Resurrection. Two thousand years are the measure of the duration of that blindness. A long time? Yes. But are we not beginning to see, as Peter, his brother disciples, and Paul at last saw clearly, the divine Man in our midst, central to all human experience? That divine Man is the Christ of God, whose image and likeness we bear—the image of the deathless Man, eternal in the heavens.

PRAYER

God of the living, and not of the dead, who hast given us mortal bodies that through them we may possess a spiritual body which the Master brought back from death to prove our everlasting inheritance, to Thee we draw near, praying for that knowledge of ourselves which leads to an understanding of the law of conscious immortality. May we be lifted above that which is temporal to that which is eternal. May we be lifted from death to life by the cross on which our Master died. We believe that it is Thy will that we should inherit all things even as Jesus inherited them. We know that inheritance without understanding is an evil; hence our life here.

Give us strength to walk the rest of the road, looking unto Jesus, the author and finisher of our faith. We thank Thee for our companionship with him. Though we, too, have sold him for copper and silver and gold, and though we have betrayed him through our thoughts as well as through our words and deeds, we look on him as our Saviour. Restore us to our rightful sonship, and keep us from leaving the path along which he went who, for the joy that was set before him, endured the cross, despising the shame.   Amen.

V

OUR POTENTIAL GODHOOD

Colossians ii : 20–iii : 4

"As you died with Christ to the Elemental spirits of the world, why live as if you still belonged to the world? Why submit to rules and regulations like 'Hands off this!' 'Taste not that!' 'Touch not this!'—referring to things that perish by being used? These rules are determined by human precepts and tenets; they get the name of 'wisdom' with their self-imposed devotions, with their fasting, with their rigorous discipline of the body, but they are of no value, they simply pamper the flesh!

"Since then you have been raised with Christ, aim at what is above, where Christ is, seated at the right hand of God; mind what is above, not what is on earth, for you died, and your life is hidden with Christ in God. When Christ, who is our life, appears, then you will appear with him in glory."

WE have two bodies, an outer and an inner

body, mortal and immortal, the one of the earth and the other of the spirit. We are of the substance of the eternal. Sometimes we call that self *the soul*, and sometimes *the spirit*, but they mean the same thing.

Man proceeds from God, and is revealed by his bodies. We are now embodied in a physical organism, with which we are familiar and have been from our first conscious moment. This organism is the natural body. It has a consciousness of its own—the carnal mind. It is the carnal mind that cries for food and drink, that grows angry, frightened, disturbed, envious, that involves us in the fulfilments of its requirements.

At best, this body lives but a little while. It is a wonderful instrument for the purpose of the soul, which comes on this planet for further instruction and must have an organism. A diver must have a body which he can put on and take off as he follows his profession. But the diver's suit is not the diver, any more than the human body is the human soul. If we could think of a diver's suit as having a mind independently of the diver, we should be able to understand the frequent sharp duality between the mortal and the spiritual man.

The mortal body has been prepared for us through the centuries of evolution, but, as we have seen, man himself—the divine man—has his origin not from the earthly but from the spiritual; man is spirit, and is passing on his way toward the fulfilment of his divine sonship. Man has arrived thus far on his road by way of this planet. In his march out of the infinite, he has passed through other planets, with other bodies, for the Spirit of God informs all things. Man as he is to-day is not the end of the soul's journey. Jesus proves that. As we look at him, we understand how much farther along the road he went. So we call him the pathfinder, the trail-maker.

These conclusions are drawn from the utterances of Paul, who speaks with high authority. He had first-hand information about the resurrection body. Jesus did not come to him, any more than he came to the first disciples, as a phantom. It was more than a vision which converted Paul. It was a direct personal experience, so profound that it turned him into a new

HIS GLORIOUS BODY

way of living. Nor was Paul the only man who had this information; the writer of the Apocalypse also had it. It is our belief that the seer of Patmos was telling as best he could about the resurrection body of Jesus. It resembled a human being. It wore a long robe, with a belt of gold around its breast. Its eyes flashed like fire. Its feet glowed like burnished bronze. Its voice was like the sound of many waters. This is not a flight of poetry, but a carefully written description of the eternal Man.

If we could be divested of the outer physical body, we should resemble that eternal Man. When we meet after death, we shall resemble him. "What we are to be is not apparent yet," wrote the apostle, "but we do know that when he appears, we are to be like him—for we are to see him as he is." Our beloved who have gone before us look like that now. Do they see us as we see ourselves? No. They are conscious only of the inner spiritual body which we now have. They see us as sharing the glory which is theirs. Death is a going-on with the spiritual body to a fuller realization of divine sonship.

Take Paul's statement: "Flesh and blood

cannot inherit the Realm of God, nor can the perishing inherit the imperishable." We must not confound the physical with the spiritual body. If we could develop our spiritual bodies as Jesus did, our physical bodies would begin to manifest the power which Jesus so easily used.

But why the physical body? That is an old question and can be answered by another one: Why souls? "Foolish one," says Paul, "if you would have a harvest, you must sow and then you must reap." Life follows the law of re-embodiment, and as we sow, we shall reap. We must accept our physical bodies as the least part of us. Then sin will not reign in that body. Nothing must reign in it. It is a servant. It must not dominate us. We are to supply its needs and take the utmost care of it. It is given us as a cocoon is given to the moth and the butterfly, for protection while wings and beauty are slowly forming within.

Paul's ethic demands a full acceptance of the reality of Christ's spiritual body. Our bodies must be related to his body. So we say in the Communion service, "The Body and Blood of our Lord Jesus Christ, which were given for you, preserve your body and soul unto everlasting life." But if we accept the fact of the resurrected Jesus, we must accept the fact of our resurrection, too. We must be risen now. Why wait for the episode of death—a little and unimportant pageant? We must enter eternity now. If Jesus overcame death, he overcame it for us.

We must bear about in our bodies the marks, not of his death, but of his Resurrection. They are the marks of his glory. We deny that glory when we yield to the tyranny of sorrow and care. Roll away the stone from the door of the tomb—roll it away!

Christianity began with the Resurrection, not with the cross. We must be crucified that we may be resurrected. We must crucify the old man, the outer earth man, the old animal consciousness, that we may share the Resurrection of Jesus. This was in the thought of Paul when he wrote to the Corinthians: "If ye be risen with Christ, seek those things which are above. They are yours. Seek the things which are above the shadow of the earth and the smallness of man, for the things which are above

OUR POTENTIAL GODHOOD

belong to God, as you belong to God and God belongs to you."

PRAYER

Beloved Master, who hast said, "Blessed are the pure in heart, for they shall see God," cleanse our hearts from the defilement of physical desire. We would rise with thee and gain those things which are above these bodies of the earth. We seek the beauty of thy face and the loveliness of thy soul. We know that only as we are purified from physical desire can we see God, that God is dimmed and unreal to us when our hearts are unholy. Dear Master, we would know thee in the full power of thy Resurrection. Cleanse us from all unworthiness, that we may see thee as thou art.   Amen.

VI

GOD'S SECRET PURPOSE

I Corinthians ii (whole chapter)

"Thus when I came to you, my brothers, I did not come to proclaim to you God's secret purpose with any elaborate words or wisdom. I determined among you to be ignorant of everything except Jesus Christ, and Jesus Christ the crucified. It was in weakness and fear and with great trembling that I visited you; what I said, what I preached, did not rest on the plausible arguments of 'wisdom' but on the proof supplied by the Spirit and its power, so that your faith might not rest on any human 'wisdom' but on the power of God.

"We do discuss 'wisdom' with those who are mature; only it is not the wisdom of this world or of the dethroned Powers who rule this world, it is the mysterious Wisdom of God that we discuss, that hidden wisdom which God decreed from all eternity for our glory. None of the Powers of this world understand it (if they

had, they would never have crucified the Lord of glory). No, as it is written,

> *what no eye has ever seen,*
> *what no ear has ever heard,*
> *what never entered the mind of man,*
> *God has prepared all that for those who love him.*

And God has revealed it to us by the Spirit, for the Spirit fathoms everything, even the depths of God.

> *What human being can understand the thoughts of a man,*
>   *except the man's own inner spirit?*
> *So too no one understands the thoughts of God,*
>   *except the Spirit of God.*

Now we have received the Spirit—not the spirit of the world but the Spirit that comes from God, that we may understand what God bestows upon us. And this is what we discuss, using language taught by no human wisdom but by the Spirit. We interpret what is spiritual in spiritual language. The unspiritual man rejects these truths of the Spirit of God; to him they are 'sheer folly,' he cannot understand them. And the reason is, that they must be read with the spiritual eye. The spiritual man, again, can read the meaning of everything; and yet no one can read what he is. For who ever understood the thoughts of the Lord, so as to give him instruction? No one. Well, our thoughts are Christ's thoughts."

IMAGINE being in Corinth somewhere around the year 54 and listening to this letter being read for the first time. And imagine having known the man who wrote it. The Corinthians had seen and heard him. He had converted them by his message and they had given up their hearts to him. How irresistible the man was! He had new information about God, with an unusual power of speech. He stood before them, vital, sincere, telling of the death of a Man on a cross and of his Resurrection from a tomb.

Imagine being in the group who received this letter, written some time after his departure. We should probably be uncomfortable, as the Corinthians were, who had split into factions over his message, taking the blessed truth which Paul had brought to them and tearing it to pieces with their debates. A group of teachers, each thinking himself superior to Paul, and claiming to have a special revelation of the mystery of Jesus and his power to save, were quarrelling among themselves, and saying bitter words. So they lost the spirit which Paul had communicated to them.

Finally Paul heard about these quarrels. It must have made him sad when he learned that his disciples were in debate over the story of the cross and the Resurrection. He wrote this letter to lead them back to first principles, back to their first lessons, back to the original glory and wonder of the gospel.

As we read this letter, we have no difficulty in describing some of these debates and the points on which the teachers differed. It is evident that the main quarrel was over the Resurrection itself; so we read: "But, some one will ask, 'how do the dead rise? What kind of body have they when they come?'" They were not satisfied to take the rose of God and wear it over their hearts; they wanted to pull the petals to pieces. Not content with the aroma of the rose, they tried to explain its scent. It is curious how some beginners toward a technic of truth reveal an impertinence of inquiry which the more profoundly experienced ones contrast by their humility. As we master our technic, we begin to understand what Jesus meant when he said to Nicodemus: "The wind blows where it wills; you can hear its sound, but you never know where it has come from or where it goes: it is the same with every one who is born of the Spirit."

We feel but we cannot explain; know but cannot describe; have but cannot trace our possession to its source.

Were the Corinthians denying the fact of the Resurrection? No; but they were trying to explain it—and quarrelling over their explanations. The four Gospels as we now have them had not yet been written, and the disciples who had experienced the Resurrection of Jesus were scattered all over the Roman world. But they were not committing their message to the written page.

Paul's claim to write with authority rested upon his assertion that he had had a personal contact with the deathless Jesus, who had commissioned him to preach the gospel. He even boasted of the fact that his ministry was directly received from the Master himself; that he did not have it from the apostles: "I told you when I came for the first time to you what I had myself received; that Christ died for our sins and conquered death; that he was seen first by Cephas, then by the twelve, then by James, then by five hundred disciples, the greater part of whom are still alive, then again by the twelve, and finally by me—who at first resisted with all my might the gospel of the Resurrection, until that day I met the living Master, who claimed me for his service."

How intimately he writes in an opening paragraph of the letter itself:

"Brothers, for the sake of our Lord Jesus Christ I beg of you all to drop these party-cries. There must be no cliques among you; you must regain your common temper and attitude. For Chloe's people inform me that you are quarrelling. By 'quarrelling' I mean that each of you has his party-cry, 'I belong to Paul,' 'And I to Apollos,' 'And I to Cephas,' 'And I to Christ.' "

The gospel, as Paul understood and gave it, began with the Resurrection, but without the cross it was incomplete. The cross was a declaration against sin. What is sin? Paul is at pains to describe it. Man is a duality, governed by a central soul—the man within. This duality consists of two bodies, an outer and an inner. Sin lies in this outer body:

> "The body is not meant for immorality but for the Lord, and the Lord is for the body; and the God who raised the Lord will also raise us by his power. Do you not know your bodies are members of Christ? Am I to take Christ's members and devote them to a harlot? Never! Do you not know that he who joins himself to a harlot is one with her in body (for the pair, it is said, shall become one flesh), while he who joins himself to the Lord is one with him in spirit. Shun immorality! Any other sin that a man commits is outside the body, but the immoral man sins against his body. Do you not know your body is the temple of the holy Spirit within you— the Spirit you have received from God? You are not your own, you were bought for a price; then glorify God with your body."

It is in the flesh body that sin works. Is then the body unholy? No. But the peril of that body is in its consciousness which appears to be independent of the soul or spirit. What is that consciousness? An ancestral memory. Every cell of that body is an embodiment of racial experiences. It is overgrown with jungles, flooded with the passion of old battles. It

GOD'S SECRET PURPOSE

is a colony of animal impulses, a coral reef builded of dead and ancient forms of life.

Sin appears when these impulses clash with the eternal memory of the soul. By submitting to these impulses in place of the soul's memory, we fall into sin. On the other hand, the spiritual body is compounded of those memories which the soul has gathered upon its way. All the high impulses of the ages of that journey have gone into the making of the spiritual body. This constitutes the struggle between the animal and the spiritual body. The resurrection of the soul appears when the lower memories are subordinated to the higher memories.

Jesus had crucified his lower body years before he climbed to the cross. This, according to Paul, measures the value of the cross to the Master's disciples. So, in quarrelling at Corinth over the mode of the Resurrection, they were losing the inheritance of its spiritual power through descent into sin. The moment they began to dispute among themselves concerning the method of God, they separated themselves from the power of its working. They could not know the power of the Resurrection until they had mastered the power of the cross. They must begin by casting out sin, and their quarrellings were evidence to the fact that they had not crucified their mortal bodies. They were living within the labyrinths of the jungle. They were not raising palms from their coral islands. They were going back to the memories of those lesser forms submerged beneath an ancient sea.

The power of the Resurrection is won as we forsake the jungle and the coral reef. We must be dead in Christ that we may be risen with him. The cross is the symbol of that death, and the open tomb of that Resurrection. The natural man can never know the things of God, but the spiritual man already has them.

Imagine being in Corinth between the year 54 and 55, hearing such a letter as this. What decision should we make? That which many made when they listened to this letter: the decision to be dead unto sin and alive unto Christ, driving the stake of the cross through our mortal consciousness, that we might open it to the higher selfhood of our eternal inheritance, as the stone was rolled away from the sepulchre of Jesus.

GOD'S SECRET PURPOSE

Surely we can do this now, though centuries have passed since that letter was read to the group at Corinth. As we enter into our higher consciousness, all things will be open to us, that we may see what no mortal eye can see, hear what no mortal ear can hear, understand what no mortal mind can understand, for "what no eye has ever seen, what no ear has ever heard, what never entered the mind of man, God has prepared all that for those who love him; and God has revealed it to us by the Spirit."

PRAYER

Lead us back, O Spirit that inspired the first disciples, to him whom they knew face to face. Lead us back through all the doubts and perplexities of the ages, that we may stand in his presence to claim him as our Lord and Redeemer. Thou knowest, who searchest the thoughts of our hearts, how great is our need in this day of peril. We claim him because he has claimed us, knowing that his grace will do for us what it did for those who first received him.

May we be lifted by the challenge of his

words and changed by the beauty of his spiritual mind, recovering what we have lost in these years—the conviction that he is the Resurrection and the Life, the foundation of our faith in the unbroken companionship of all souls in the universe of God.

Lead us back to him in this hour of meditation, that for a while we may forget the outer things of the world, in that upper room of the soul where he speaks to us as he spoke of old: "Not as the world gives give I unto you. Peace. Behold it is I myself. I am yours and you are mine." Amen.

VII

MAN AND HIS FATHER

I Corinthians iii : 1–5, 9–13, 16, 17, 21

"*But I could not discuss things with you, my brothers, as spiritual persons; I had to address you as worldlings, as mere babes in Christ. I fed you with milk, not with solid food. You were not able for solid food, and you are not able even now; you are still worldly. For with jealousy and quarrels in your midst, are you not worldly, are you not behaving like ordinary men? When one cries, 'I belong to Paul,' and another, 'I belong to Apollos,' what are you but men of the world? Who is Apollos? Who is Paul? They are simply used by God to give you faith, each as the Lord assigns his task.*

"*We work together in God's service; you are God's field to be planted, God's house to be built. In virtue of my commission from God, I laid the foundation of the house like an expert master-builder. It remains for another to build*

HIS GLORIOUS BODY

on this foundation. Whoever he is, let him be careful how he builds. The foundation is laid, namely Jesus Christ, and no one can lay any other. On that foundation anyone may build gold, silver, precious stones, wood, hay, or straw, but in every case the nature of his work will come out; the Day will show what it is, for the Day breaks in fire, and the fire will test the work of each, no matter what that work may be.

"Do you not know you are God's temple and that God's Spirit dwells within you? God will destroy anyone who would destroy God's temple, for God's temple is sacred—and that is what you are.

"So you must not boast about men. For all belongs to you; Paul, Apollos, Cephas, the world, life, death, the present and the future—all belongs to you; and you belong to Christ, and Christ to God."

We have sat in Corinth, listening to a letter which had just come from Ephesus. In Corinth we found the party factions and foolish quarrels that disturb us in this hour. What power is dissipated in these factions and quarrels arising out of things which we can never know; for the ways of God are past finding out.

But there is one thing that we can know and must never forget: that God and man meet as Father and son. When a son denies his father, communion is impossible. We frequently do that by thinking of ourselves as physical bodies, giving reality to jungle memories.

This is the substance of the letter that came from Ephesus to Corinth. How it insists that the natural man cannot understand spiritual things; that only as our consciousness changes from our physical to our spiritual selfhood can we talk with God. Conversion is a changing from the physical to the spiritual state of embodiment; is the discovery that, as there is a natural, so there is a spiritual body.

And how this letter makes us ashamed of ourselves! Like the Corinthians, we have refused to claim our eternal inheritance. We, too, must see that Jesus died to prove that we can live forever. The body that died on the cross and the body that came forth from the tomb were two bodies, owned by the one divine selfhood of the Master. The body that died on the cross came into existence by birth, was inherited from the earth out of which it was fashioned. The body that left the tomb and appeared to the first disciples and then to Paul, was inherited from God, not created but begotten, and of the same substance with the Father, as all spiritual bodies are—the body of the divine eternal Man:

"Man the first is from the earth, material; Man the second is from heaven. As Man the material is, so are the material; as Man the heavenly is, so are the heavenly. Thus, as we have borne the likeness of material Man, so are we to bear the likeness of the heavenly Man. I tell you this, my brothers, flesh and blood cannot inherit the Realm of God, nor can the perishing inherit the imperishable."

This profound truth explains the old quarrel which we are still continuing. What a wonderful thing it would be if, at the next General Convention, the Presiding Bishop were to read this letter as it was read for the first time at Corinth! Should we not kneel in silent prayer and then return to the Master's work in a new spirit? How it would change the entire character of the Church; and how it would solve the problem of foreign and domestic missions. If we could stimulate the young genius of America to realize the implications of this letter, we should have a new ministry of power and consecration.

We need to recapture the mood of the synagogue at Corinth when this letter was read for the first time, and to ponder this truth: "Your bodies are the temples of God. You are an embodiment of God. All that was embodied in the Man Jesus is in you." One day the Church of Jesus will kneel before this message, and then there will be no difficulty about the reunion of Christendom; all believers will find themselves one in the truth that God is seeking now to be manifested through His sons, who, by yielding their physical bodies as Jesus did—as Paul was trying to do—will hold their ground against the arrogance of the carnal mind, abounding in the work of the Lord, knowing that their labor for him can never be thrown away.

But there is a difficulty in the way—a difficulty which has met all the disciples of Jesus from the beginning. This is the difficulty: How can we, in a world like this, overcome the habit of this flesh body? There is an answer, and Paul has given it. Let us take it out of its conventional setting and make it as intimate and as modern as we can:

"Brother, I count not myself yet to have fully attained the freedom of the spiritual body. The other body is still clamorous and in the way. But I am training myself to forget the old animal memories which used to dominate me and interfere with the liberty of a son of God in the fulness of his spiritual body. Brother, I have seen Jesus; I have talked with him. He is always before me. And so I renew myself from day to day by following in his steps. I know as well as any man that to be physically conscious is a deadly thing. When I submit to the deceits of the former man, when I yield to the false authority of this world with its arrogance and love of display, I feel the cold finger of death on my heart. But when I follow the Master and claim with him divine sonship, then I know even as I also am known."

This confession of Paul is helpful to all who are in the path which the Master trod. We do not gain the goal in a moment, but, as we follow on, we are gladdened by a sense of increasing power. A new authority is on us; we have

MAN AND HIS FATHER

a freedom which bows to no yoke except that of obedience to him who said: "I have come that they may have life and have it to the full."

We must change our consciousness from our physical to our spiritual manhood. The physical body is a necessary but temporary instrument. We must use it as a servant. We are here with it to be trained for service to the possession of our everlasting inheritance—the resurrection body. We must overcome the fear of growing old and win the joyous realization of eternal youth. We must begin to live in our immortal manhood. We must steady our spiritual vision and understanding by the use of the physical body, setting our soul against the illusions of the flesh. We are to take the flesh body for granted. We are not to explain it away, but rise on it as on a stepping-stone to a better thing.

Let us leave the old synagogue of Corinth, with the message of our brother Paul: "Sin must not reign in your mortal bodies. Overcome that sin through the re-discovery of the soul. Be on your guard against the enemy who deceives the eye, ear, and tongue with the illusions of matter. Die with Jesus and resurrect with Christ."

PRAYER

O Builder and Maker of houses not made with hands, give us at this hour the true knowledge of ourselves as temples of Thine indwelling presence, that we may make our physical bodies servants of that inner Guest whose light shines through into all the world. Help us to raise the physical to the spiritual, keeping under our bodies and raising them to Thee who art the very God incarnated in us and waiting to pour upon the world the glory of our risen Master. When we are tempted to the ignoble use of our lower bodies, may we remember Thee, O invisible Guest, so that we may live and walk as companions of him who said: "But I, when I am lifted up from the earth, will draw all men to myself." Amen.

VIII

THE POWER OF THE RESURRECTION

Philippians iii : 7–16

"But for Christ's sake I have learned to count my former gains a loss; indeed I count anything a loss, compared to the supreme value of knowing Christ Jesus my Lord. For his sake I have lost everything (I count it all the veriest refuse) in order to gain Christ and be found at death in him, possessing no legal righteousness of my own but the righteousness of faith in Christ, the divine righteousness that rests on faith. I would know him in the power of his resurrection and the fellowship of his sufferings, with my nature transformed to die as he died, to see if I too can attain the resurrection from the dead. Not that I have already attained this or am already perfect, but I press forward to appropriate it, because I have been appropriated myself by Christ Jesus. Brothers, I for one do not consider myself to have appropriated this; my one thought is, by forgetting what lies

behind me and straining to what lies before me, to press on to the goal for the prize of God's high call in Christ Jesus. For all those of our number who are mature, this must be the point of view; God will reveal that to any of you who look at things differently. Only, we must let our steps be guided by such truth as we have attained."

The man who wrote these words had failed to find God in the religion of his youth. From his boyhood to the time of his conversion, he had passionately hungered and thirsted for the knowledge of God. But that knowledge was denied him, because he believed that God was a Judge with laws to be obeyed. If one disobeyed those laws, the Judge would be angry. If one obeyed them, the Judge would be gracious and kind.

So he cried: "Miserable wretch that I am! Who will rescue me from this body of death?" There was no response to that cry until he learned that God is not a Judge nor a King, but a Father and a Friend who is closer than a brother. With the exception of a few of the prophets, nobody but Jesus seems to have thought of applying to human nature these words: "Let us make man divine." The Scribes and Pharisees had speculated about these words, but they seem never to have grasped their implications. To them the image and likeness of God described man's immortality won by a literal obedience to the Mosaic code. When they brought a sinful woman to Jesus, they quoted Moses. Jesus replied, "Let the innocent among you throw the first stone at her." And once when he healed a man on the Sabbath day, they again quoted Moses. Jesus answered: "The sabbath was made for man, not man for the sabbath."

When Paul first heard of Jesus, he opposed him by persecuting his disciples. Still believing that God was a Judge, he regarded Jesus himself as a blasphemous and evil man. To this he confessed when he declared: "I once believed it my duty indeed actively to oppose the name of Jesus the Nazarene."

Then there came a day when Paul and Jesus met. How could they meet when Jesus had died on a cross? There have been many answers to this question. One of the most popular is Renan's: "The Christ who gives him [Paul] personal revelations is his own phantom,—it is himself he hears, while thinking he hears Jesus."

Since that explanation has already been met, we pass it by without further comment. Renan, who failed to understand Jesus and whose life of the Master is one of the most beautiful, and least convincing, of the many attempts to account for the Galilean, could hardly be expected to understand the greatest of the apostles.

A more convincing answer is in the theory that Paul, in going on his way to Damascus, was haunted by the beautiful face of the dying Stephen and his plea, "Lord, let not this sin stand against them!" He was further haunted by memories of those whom he had imprisoned for their faith in the resurrected Jesus, and suddenly came to his senses by an inrush of divine illumination.

This is one of the most popular and convincing answers to the question: How did Paul and Jesus meet? For we are bound to have difficulty about the story of the open tomb.

THE POWER OF THE RESURRECTION

There are so many obvious contradictions in the accounts given by the four Evangelists that it is not easy to accept them as literal history. Ingenious explanations have been offered, which derive from this second interpretation of what happened on the road to Damascus. Because Mark's description of a young man at the open tomb is contradicted by Luke telling in detail of two angels sitting there, many have concluded that the Easter story was created by a pious imagination.

To show how far men have gone in their attempt to escape the challenge of the open tomb, a theory is still current that the man Jesus lived some fifty years before the era to which he gave his name. This man was a pious young Jew, who died obscurely for his faith in his people. After his death, a tradition began to take hold of the generation following him. This tradition witnesses to the longing of Israel for a Messiah who would save his nation now trembling into ruin. And when that nation fell before the armies of Titus, the story of this young Jew, whose name was Jehoshua, so fired the imagination of a group of frustrated pa-

HIS GLORIOUS BODY

triots that the New Testament story began to take shape in their minds.

Set aside these labored efforts to account for the fact which Paul declares to be true, and begin with an analysis of the man who proclaimed it in all his letters. Come face to face with Paul. Do we know of a greater man? Are we not in the presence of an unusual genius? His letters surely reveal that. We conclude that the authority of this genius, combined with the acknowledged sincerity of his life, justifies our faith in the truth of his repeated statement: "Jesus conquered death."

The Philippian letter has been chosen for this meditation because it reveals the rare humility of Paul, who speaks as a student to his fellows, saying in substance:

"I have been talking to you a lot about this spiritual body. Lest some of you might think that I have fully possessed this body, let me tell you that I have not done so. I am still a defeated and frustrated man. But what a goal is set before us! Think, one day we shall be lifted above the tyranny of the physical body, to the glory of the liberty of the sons of God."

THE POWER OF THE RESURRECTION

Let us join Paul in the adventure toward the possession of the resurrection body. We must not be discouraged because that body is difficult to win. But if we would win it, we must stop harking back to our failures. We must forget what lies behind. We must get rid of negatives. We are to walk no more through the valley of the shadow of death. Jesus has led us through that valley to the still waters of understanding.

Remorse is not repentance. Remorse is fettered by carnal memories. We must break those fetters and walk in freedom with those who have accepted the risen Master. We are heirs of his spiritual body which he revealed in time to those who followed him, as he will reveal it to us if we are faithful.

We have been forgiven, as he forgave the woman in the temple and the man at the pool of Siloam. Let us begin with that forgiveness and with the knowledge that the pardon of one who understands and knows us better than we understand and know ourselves has been pronounced over us. Let us forget what lies behind. Acknowledging our sin, let us go forth in gladness to the fight for eternal life which we are waging against jungle memories; for it is written: "The conqueror shall obtain this, and I will be his God, and he shall be my son."

Do not waste your time in worry and idle regret. When those hours of despondency and depression are upon you, look unto Jesus, remembering that he keeps his promise: "I am with you always."

He will make himself known to us if we are courageous and strong, and will say to us what he said to Paul: "Go on. Do not be discouraged. Struggle, wrestle, fight; for my strength is made perfect in your acknowledgment of carnal weakness. One day you shall be lifted with me and possess all that I have won for your sakes."

PRAYER

Master Jesus, thou hast called us out of the carnal into the spiritual mind. We would obey thee but are troubled by the difficulties that are in the way. Old habits of thought still cling to us and we see as in a mirror. Like the disciples who betrayed, denied, and deserted thee, we also have sinned, not because we do not love thee, but because we are still weak and untrained. The world of matter and of time presses heavily on us. There are moments when we rise above this world and find ourselves at peace with thee in the spiritual world. In those moments of illumination, we know that the spiritual world is the real one. Then we return to earth and are absorbed in our cares and conceits. In this we betray, deny, and desert thee. We return to thee when we dare to believe in the story of thy victory over death.

We turn to thee at this hour and ask for guidance in the days that are before us. Guide and comfort us. Give us a deepening sense of thy comradeship that we may forget what lies behind and press toward the mark, God's prize in thy life and all that thou art. Thou hast the words of eternal life; thou art the true bread that comes down from heaven. May we eat of that bread and never die. Cover us with thy mercy and forgiveness. Renew in us a right spirit that we may be ministers and stewards of thy mysteries. Amen.

IX

PAUL AND PETER
Galatians i : 11–19

"Brothers, I tell you the gospel that I preach is not a human affair; no man put it into my hands, no man taught me what it meant, I had it by a revelation of Jesus Christ. You know the story of my past career in Judaism; you know how furiously I persecuted the church of God and harried it, and how I outstripped many of my own age and race in my special ardour for the ancestral traditions of my house. But the God who had set me apart from my very birth called me by his grace, and when he chose to reveal his Son to me, that I might preach him to the Gentiles, instead of consulting with any human being, instead of going up to Jerusalem to see those who had been apostles before me, I went off at once to Arabia, and on my return I came back to Damascus. Then, after three years, I went up to Jerusalem to make the acquaintance of Cephas. I stayed a

fortnight with him. I saw no other apostle, only James the brother of the Lord."

There are two methods of studying the New Testament. One is through the mind of the centuries of theological interpretation. The other is to ignore that interpretation and consult the first disciples.

According to the theological interpretation, the disciples looked for a literal coming of Jesus out of the sky with an army of angels about him. He would come with the sound of a trumpet, calling the dead from the earth and the sea. At the first blast of that trumpet, the saved would arise to meet their Lord in the air, standing at the right side of Jesus on his throne; and at the second blast, the damned would take their place at the left side of that throne, waiting for their eternal doom.

Even many critics of the New Testament have accepted this interpretation of the apostolic hope concerning the second coming of Jesus. So they laugh at Paul, using his words literally: "The trumpet will sound, the dead will rise imperishable, and we shall be changed."

They blame him for crystallizing the vague apocalyptic expectations of the original group, tracing these expectations to Jesus himself who, they say, died on the cross under the delusion that he would rise again and later come with glory to judge the earth.

By the second method, we go beyond the literature of the New Testament. We are confronted at once with two possibilities: either Jesus was superior to his disciples, and therefore beyond their understanding of his teaching; or he was a literary creation of their emotional reactions to the sudden catastrophe of Golgotha. It is here where we must make our decision. As we study the words of Jesus, however they may be changed in the narratives forming the body of the four Gospels, we are aware of such an altitude of thought and understanding that we are constrained to say with Peter: "Thou hast the words of eternal life." Then we turn to the Gospels and the Acts of the Apostles with a new sympathy for the men who bravely undertook the difficult task of describing their Master to those who had not met him.

consciously literary. Perhaps that is the reason why they are such wonderful letters. How conversational, how intimate, how close to us! There is on them the freshness of the lilies which grew in the garden of the Resurrection.

These letters, which we are studying with growing enthusiasm, take us back to the morning of the day of Jesus. They tell us that twenty-five years after the Master's death, the first disciples were saying that the cross explained the Old Testament and that the Resurrection from the dead had called them to a new way of living. It is through these letters that we are able to look on the face of Simon, whom Jesus called a rock.

In the Galatian letter, Paul tells us some very definite things about himself and Peter. Let us try to recapture the conversation that must have passed in the course of that fortnight when Paul was Peter's guest at Jerusalem. What would be the subject of their conversation?

Some scholars have tried to prove that Paul worked altogether independently of the first disciples, that he tore the religion of Jesus entirely out of its beautiful setting of simplicity and fashioned it into a synthetic philosophy of Asiatic, Semitic, and Latin speculations. But if Paul told the truth when he wrote to the Galatians—and Renan includes this letter among the authentic writings of the apostle—then three years after his conversion, and possibly five years after the crucifixion, he and Peter talked together about Jesus—his life, his death, his Resurrection. It is unthinkable that these two men met to fabricate a myth of the cross and the open tomb. Their lives repudiate that theory. Surely we stand on a certainty when we cross the bridge which Paul has built for us to early moments with the first disciples of our Master.

Let us cross that bridge and listen as Paul and Peter talk. Naturally Peter would be suspicious of Paul. Could he forget the man who had harried the disciples? Yet, on the other hand, he had heard the story of what had happened near the gate of Damascus, and could not help kindling toward the new convert.

Why was Paul Peter's guest? Because they shared one experience: they had met the risen Lord. That experience drew them together and

ligions of Egypt, Persia, and India; and we know that Jerusalem was in ferment of many debates over the matter. But Christianity differs from these religions in this: Jesus was not like Socrates or Buddha who gave to their disciples a philosophy of the soul. There is little philosophy of that kind in the recorded words of our Master. He stands unique among the Masters, not as a teacher but as a demonstrator of the truth which one of the apocryphal writers enshrined in a sentence: "God created man to be immortal."

The Master never dodged any of the questions raised by his opponents. His parable of the rich man and Lazarus is an indication of what was in his mind. Yet how little he had to say about what happens after death. Why? Because that question was no problem to him. Birth and death were episodes in the eternal life of the soul. His answer to the Pharisees has been misunderstood: "I have existed before Abraham was born." In this he laid no claim to an eternity which others lacked. He asserted it for us all.

We have failed the Master and have distorted

his teaching by making too much of death. Death is softened under his spell. It is an event to be met by the ever-living soul which conquers death as it becomes one with the Father. This Jesus proved by his Resurrection, as he had already indicated it when he said: "I have come that they may have life and have it to the full."

Granting this, we can understand how hard it was for the first disciples to account for the experience of the open tomb. It swept them off their feet. The story of the Emmaus walk is one of the most beautiful, as it is one of the most authentic, stories of the post-resurrection manifestations. We have made the point, which we again make here, that whatever the disciples thought about survival, it did not help them to understand the Resurrection.

Let us place ourselves with Paul on the road to Damascus. He represents all the vague thinking about survival so characteristic of his age. By his own confession, which appears again and again in his letters, he was not ready for this new experience of the deathless Master. In a moment, in the twinkling of an eye, a trumpet voice sounded to him and he was changed to a new mind about himself. No wonder he was so dazed by this light that it seems for a while literally to have blinded him. The old mortal body, his ancient antagonist, was suddenly defeated by the resurrection of his spiritual manhood which had lain so long entombed in a cave of jungle memories. Thus he went staggering toward Damascus and fumbled exhausted at the door of one Judas in the Street called Straight. So we argue that the content of the Epistles, with all its ramifications, is a literary embodiment of that shattering moment when Paul heard the Master say: "I am Jesus and you persecute me."

Now we are able to understand what Paul wrote to the Galatians:

"If you are under the sway of the Spirit, you are not under the Law. Now the deeds of the flesh are quite obvious, such as sexual vice, impurity, sensuality, idolatry, magic, quarrels, dissension, jealousy, temper, rivalry, factions, party-spirit, envy, murder, drinking bouts, revelry and the like; I tell you beforehand as I have told you already, that people who indulge in such practices will never inherit the Realm of God."

How do we inherit the Realm of God? By

HIS GLORIOUS BODY

possessing our spiritual bodies. While we are under the dominion of the flesh body, denying the reality of our spiritual body, we fail to possess our divine inheritance. But when we begin to live according to the inner man, our true selfhood, the kingdom of God comes. Leaving hell behind us, we go from glory to glory. He who has so possessed his spiritual body begins to reveal its possession through its manifestation of "love, joy, peace, good temper, kindliness, generosity, fidelity, gentleness, self-control." Having crucified or overcome the old mortal body with its emotions and passions, we have become a new creation.

As time went on, this attaining of the power of the resurrection was uppermost in the thought of the first disciples. The second coming of Jesus, however it may have been obscured by their words, meant to them this spiritual attainment. Jesus did appear to them in his spiritual body. It was not like the old body, and yet it had such an identity with it that, as they developed their spiritual perceptions, they saw him as he was when he called them by the lake. They now belonged to the heaven world,

THE NEW CREATION

a spiritual colony; no longer separated from those who had died, they were spiritually present with all souls, surrounded by an innumerable company of witnesses.

What can we gather from these first witnesses? First, that the Resurrection was not a subjective experience. Listen to one whom we all love and revere, the disciple who wrote the Fourth Gospel and the letter which begins with these simple, guarded, but rapturous words:

"It is of what existed from the very beginning, of what we heard, of what we saw, of what we witnessed and touched with our own hands, it is of the Logos of Life (the Life has appeared; we saw it, we testify to it, we bring you word of that eternal Life which existed with the Father and was disclosed to us)—it is of what we heard and saw that we bring you word, so that you may share our fellowship; and our fellowship is with the Father and with his Son Jesus Christ. We are writing this to you that our own joy may be complete."

All the learning of the ages drifts like sand before the breath of the spirit which inspires this direct statement from this man who was convinced of the truth about which he wrote. There are no exaggerations, no attempts to explain. The unalterable fact of the Resurrection is before the man who says: "We saw, we testified, we bring you word that you may share our fellowship."

Second, there is a world of spiritual reality to which we belong. The door to that world is an open tomb. As we pass through that door, we are released from the bondage of the flesh, strengthened by Christ in the inner man, who "will transform the body that belongs to our low estate till it resembles the body of his Glory, by the same power that enables him to make everything subject to himself."

Third, the gospel of the Resurrection demands a changed mind of those who receive it. Christianity is a technic of the new life which Jesus revealed when he rose from the dead.

Finally, wherever the Church has preached that gospel, it has been a power for salvation to men. Only as we who belong to that Church share with the first disciples the fellowship of the Resurrection, can we turn humanity from the bondage of the flesh into the liberty of the glory of the children of God.

THE NEW CREATION

PRAYER

Lord of eternal life and God of our salvation, fix our hearts upon him who for all mankind died on the cross and rose again from the dead. Inspire us by Thy pure Spirit to receive what the gospel offers us. Cleanse us from the iniquities of the flesh which blind us to the truth, hardening our hearts against its challenge. We would be witnesses of the Resurrection, sons of its fellowship, and stewards of its mystery.

If, by sorrow and bereavement of death, we falter before the tomb, then roll away its stone, that we may discover the emptiness of the old illusion which has held us so long in its power. Teach us to crucify the former man that we may share with the Master the new creation according to the mighty power whereby he is able to subdue all things unto himself.   Amen.

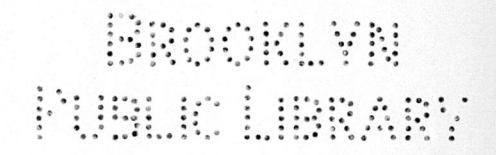

XI

OUR GLORIOUS BODY

Ephesians i : 1–14

"Paul, by the will of God an apostle of Jesus Christ, to the saints who are faithful in Jesus Christ: grace and peace to you from God our Father and the Lord Jesus Christ.

"Blessed be the God and Father of our Lord Jesus Christ who in Christ has blessed us with every spiritual blessing! He chose us in him ere the world was founded, to be consecrated and unblemished in his sight, destining us in love to be his sons through Jesus Christ. Such was the purpose of his will, redounding to the praise of his glorious grace bestowed on us in the Beloved, in whom we enjoy our redemption, the forgiveness of our trespasses, by the blood he shed. So richly has God lavished his grace upon us! He has granted us complete insight and understanding of the open secret of his will, showing us how it was the purpose of his design so to order it in the fulness of the ages that all things in heaven and earth alike should *be gathered up in Christ—in the Christ in whom we have had our heritage allotted us (as was decreed in the design of him who carries out everything according to the counsel of his will), to make us redound to the praise of his glory by being the first to put our hope in Christ. You also have heard the message of the truth, the gospel of your salvation, and in him you also by your faith have been stamped with the seal of the long-promised holy Spirit which is the pledge and instalment of our common heritage, that we may obtain our divine possession and so redound to the praise of his glory."*

THESE are profound words—profound to the point of obscurity—in this age that has manufactured "clear thinking," delighting in the obvious strenuously and startlingly explained: an age of people who have lost the gift of imagination, an age of the journalist, of the epigram and the little, soulless poem, an age of the short story and of logic.

We shall never understand what lies within the words we have chosen while we demand the simple, the clear, and the obvious. Einstein is said to be the profoundest thinker in the world of physics. Only a few can understand him; yet the generations of the future will probably think in terms of what he has written on a few pages. Paul was as new and as profound in his age as Einstein is in ours. The really deep things cannot easily be clarified or made simple. The so-called "clear thinker" is not necessarily deep, accurate, original.

We have seen that Christianity began with the experience of the first disciples with the cross and the open tomb. What an experience! Who could measure it? Peter and John spent the rest of their lives in a continuous effort to explain it to the world. Read the Gospel according to St. Mark and see how Peter, who is behind its testimony, shrank from talking about the open tomb. It is significant that this Gospel breaks off suddenly, as though Peter could tell no more. John, in his old age, looking back to the cross and the tomb, wrote at greater length and with a clearer understanding of their meaning. That is why his Gospel grows upon us as we study it through the ripening years of our own discipleship.

We value the letters of Paul because he was the first to probe the depths and the heights of the mystery of the cross and the tomb. The opening words of this letter are quite within the scope of his thought, and for that reason we ascribe it to Paul. Only such an intellect could have faced the problems which this letter attempts to solve, and it reveals Paul at his highest. It is interesting to compare this letter with the one which he wrote to the Thessalonians after he had visited them on his way to Corinth. How the man had matured since those first days, when, having come out of Arabia, he was thinking his way to the conclusions embodied in the Ephesian letter, measuring the height, the depth, the length, and the breadth of the cross and of the Resurrection.

Though Paul is never identified with the idiom of the Fourth Gospel, its thought is in harmony with the thought of Paul to such an extent that it has been suggested that John derived some of his thinking from Paul. A comparison between the two makes this theory almost convincing:

"Blessed be the God and Father of our Lord Jesus

Christ who in Christ has blessed us with every spiritual blessing! He chose us in him ere the world was founded, to be consecrated and unblemished in his sight, destining us in love to be his sons through Jesus Christ. Such was the purpose of his will, redounding to the praise of his glorious grace bestowed on us in the Beloved, in whom we enjoy our redemption, the forgiveness of our trespasses, by the blood he shed. So richly has God lavished his grace upon us! He has granted us complete insight and understanding of the open secret of his will, showing us how it was the purpose of his design so to order it in the fulness of the ages that all things in heaven and earth alike should be gathered up in Christ."

So Paul began his letter to the Ephesians. And as a prologue to his Gospel, John wrote this:

"The Logos existed in the very beginning,
the Logos was with God,
the Logos was divine.
He was with God in the very beginning:
through him all existence came into being,
no existence came into being apart from him.
In him life lay,
and this life was the Light for men:
amid the darkness the Light shone,
but the darkness did not master it."

Let us change the word "Logos" and read as follows, in a rough paraphrase of the Gospel:

OUR GLORIOUS BODY

"In the beginning was the plan of God. Whatever God caused to be was in harmony with that plan." What was the plan? By returning to the Ephesian letter, we find that according to Paul it was this:

"May the God of our Lord Jesus Christ, the glorious Father, grant you the Spirit of wisdom and revelation for the knowledge of himself, illuminating the eyes of your heart so that you can understand the hope to which He calls us, the wealth of his glorious heritage in the saints, and the surpassing greatness of his power over us believers—a power which operates with the strength of the might which he exerted in raising Christ from the dead and seating him at his right hand in the heavenly sphere, above all the angelic Rulers, Authorities, Powers, and Lords, above every Name that is to be named not only in this age but in the age to come—he has put everything under his feet and set him as head over everything for the church, the church which is his Body, filled by him who fills the universe entirely. . . .

"This grace was vouchsafed me, that I should bring the Gentiles the gospel of the fathomless wealth of Christ and enlighten all men upon the new order of that divine secret which God the Creator of all concealed from eternity—intending to let the full sweep of the divine wisdom be disclosed now by the church to the angelic Rulers and Authorities in the heavenly sphere, in terms of the eternal purpose [plan—Logos] which he has realized in Christ Jesus our Lord, through whom, as we have faith in him, we enjoy our confidence of free access. . . .

[103]

HIS GLORIOUS BODY

"For this reason, then, I kneel before the Father from whom every family in heaven and on earth derives its name and nature, praying Him out of the wealth of his glory to grant you a mighty increase of strength by his Spirit in the inner man. May Christ dwell in your hearts as you have faith! . . . May you be filled with the entire fulness of God!"

Paul was among the first to see that when Jesus came, God said: "It is finished." The plan was completed!

We also have the witness of the letter to the Romans. How it bears upon what we have been pondering together:

"Present suffering, I hold, is a mere nothing compared to the glory that we are to have revealed. Even the creation waits with eager longing for the sons of God to be revealed. For creation was not rendered futile by its own choice, but by the will of Him who thus made it subject, the hope being that creation as well as man would one day be freed from its thraldom to decay and gain the glorious freedom of the children of God."

Is not this the thought of the Epistle to the Ephesians? To Paul the importance of Jesus was in more than his life and death and Resurrection. Jesus is a declaration of the Logos or

OUR GLORIOUS BODY

plan of God for the human race. Jesus was not an afterthought of God. He came in his order, as he said: "I have not come to destroy the Law but to fulfill it." He came because God, from the beginning, was working toward the manifestation of all His sons. Jesus is a pledge of that manifestation. Through him man has now entered into his divine sonship.

Jesus is the first-fruits of those who slept. What was that sleep? Paul answered that question when he wrote to the Corinthians: "How are the dead raised up, and with what body do they come?" The following paraphrase is offered to clear up a difficult passage: "In order that there may be life, there must be a planting, and that which is planted must die that it may come to the harvest. That is God's way with men as well with plants. We are sown animate bodies when we are born into them. We are reaped spiritual bodies when the animate dies."

We were born animate bodies. We must now be born spiritual bodies by the death of the animate body. What is the death of the animate body? Paul has answered for us: "By overcoming hate, fear, sexual impulses, and every form of carnal selfishness. Drive the stake of our Master's cross through the carnal mind, and rise from the dead to share with him the resurrection to eternal life."

PRAYER

Strong Son of God, immortal Love revealed in human form that the infinite purpose of the Father concerning us might be revealed, to thee we come in gladness, knowing that by faith we are one with thee in that body of which thou art the head.

We would know thy love in its height, piercing the highest dream of God; in its depth, daring the uttermost darkness of that experience which ends in the knowledge of Him whom to know is life eternal. We would know thy love in its breadth, wide as the arms of thy cross, the symbol of that universal brotherhood which all nations will share as they follow thee. We would know its length, measuring the path of all souls on their way through mortal birth to spiritual attainment.

Open our vision and deepen our understanding that the light of the eternal plan may shine upon our faces in the glory which we had with thee and the Father before the world was. Amen.

XII

SPIRITUAL ATHLETICS

Ephesians iii : 14–19

"For this reason, then, I kneel before the Father from whom every family in heaven and on earth derives its name and nature, praying Him out of the wealth of his glory to grant you a mighty increase of strength by his Spirit in the inner man. May Christ dwell in your hearts as you have faith! May you be so fixed and founded in love that you can grasp with all the saints what is the meaning of 'the Breadth,' 'the Length,' 'the Depth,' and 'the Height,' by knowing the love of Christ which surpasses all knowledge!"

ONE of the many values in Paul's letters is in their communication to us of his spiritual technic. The prayer which we have read describes that technic. Paul can never be understood if we study him only in relation to an experience which changed him from a Pharisee to a Christian. We must also study him as he struggled with that experience, seeking to relate it to the new life which began with his conversion.

In a word, Paul's spiritual technic is prayer. Prayer—what is it? If we could fully answer that question, what gain would be ours! We must face some of the theories of prayer before we can hope to clear our minds of the cant which has rendered the word itself so unpalatable to the multitudes who mock at prayer. Why? Because, when they pray, God does not answer them. God cannot answer them because they approach Him in fear. Many people are afraid to live and afraid to die. They look on God as a powerful King who gives or withholds according to His whim. They think of God as Caliban thought of Setebos:

> "He is strong and Lord.
> Am strong myself compared to yonder crabs
> That march now from the mountain to the sea;
> Let twenty pass, and stone the twenty-first,
> Loving not, hating not, just choosing so.
> Say, the first straggler that boasts purple spots
> Shall join the file, one pincer twisted off;
> Say, this bruised fellow shall receive a worm,

And two worms he whose nippers end in red;
As it likes me each time, I do: so He."

True prayer is never like that, and the reason why people abandon prayer is because they think of the God and Father of us all as Caliban thought of Setebos, his mother's God. Notice, *his mother's God*—not Caliban's God. He had not found Him as a son finds his father. Here we have described those theories of prayer which are wrong and futile because they do not begin with "Our Father." "When you pray," said Jesus, "call God *Father*."

The experience which changed Paul from a Pharisee to a Christian taught him how to pray. He began with the assertion of his divine sonship. God was his Father and, as a son, he conferred with Him about the new life which he had found through Jesus. But that new life must be firmly established in his thought. This would not be easy: when he would do good, evil was present with him. To set himself against the dominion of the former man required steady, hard, and courageous thinking.

Prayer is a steadfast resistance against the tyranny of a former way of living. This tyr-

SPIRITUAL ATHLETICS

anny has already been described. We pray as we resist the intrusion of the carnal mind in all our relationships with life. The carnal mind knocks at one door—the door of fear. "Why are ye fearful?" said Jesus. It must have been hard for him to understand this habit of fearfulness in the minds of his disciples to whom he had given a prayer which began: "Our Father who art in heaven."

We resist the carnal mind by shutting the only door by which it can enter upon the life of the inner man—fear. We overcome fear by thought. How? Paul answers: "As you renew your thought. Make it vigorous. Keep it active. Practise that activity at all times. Never cease in this practice." When he was writing to the Corinthians, he said:

"Do you not know that in a race, though all run, only one man gains the prize? Run so as to win the prize. Every athlete practises self-restraint all round; but while they do it to win a fading wreath, we do it for an unfading. Well, I run without swerving; I do not plant my blows upon the empty air—no, I maul and master my body, in case, after preaching to other people, I am disqualified myself."

How sturdy the soul of this man was, and

what implications are carried to us in this description of spiritual athletics. Prayer is a mental application of the principles of the new life upon which we enter when we accept Jesus as our Master. Again we hear Paul say: "Brothers, do not be children in the sphere of intelligence. In evil be mere infants, but be mature in your intelligence"—as also we hear him say with a shout of joy: "The victory is ours, thank God! He makes it ours by our Lord Jesus Christ. . . . Hold your ground, immovable; abound in work for the Lord at all times, for you may be sure that in the Lord your labor is never thrown away."

"In the Lord"—is not this another way of saying "strengthened by Christ in the inner man"? We are called to the inheritance of our spiritual manhood. Prayer is more than a struggle to possess that manhood. It includes the development of our consciousness of that inheritance. Begin with to-day. Do not be afraid to say within yourself: "I am a son of God and a brother of Jesus. I believe in the communion of the holy ones. I too am holy if I centre my consciousness in the soul."

SPIRITUAL ATHLETICS

When we think of our irregular discipleship—its contradictions, perversities, pathetic weaknesses—it is not easy to set ourselves toward the acquisition of this spiritual technic which is called prayer. Have we not said to ourselves: "I am so inconsistent. One moment I am up and away with the Master, and the next I am back again into the sordid details of worry, care, jealousy, hatred, and stupid ineffectiveness"? We must meet that as all beginners meet their failures, with a fair understanding of the acknowledged difficulties which are in the path of those who strive toward any goal.

Certain tests with which we are all familiar may be of value here. Begin with the start of the day. We open our eyes upon a gloomy and unhappy world, troubled with dreams that would not let us rest. We arise despondent. How can one begin the day as a son of God with an aching head or with throbbing nerves that send messages of pain to every member of the physical body?

Prayer begins that moment when we face this troublesome body with the happiness, the peace, and the health of our inner manhood. Command that body and say to it: "In spite of your groaning and complaining, you must serve me this day. I have a work to do and I will do it with all my might."

Paul takes us into his confidence concerning this test by telling us about his poor, aching body that troubled him with its complaining until at last he talked about it to Jesus. "Three times over," he says, "I prayed the Lord to make it leave me, but he told me, 'It is enough for you to have my grace: it is in weakness that [my] power is fully felt.' So I am proud to boast of all my weakness, and thus to have the power of Christ resting on my life. It makes me satisfied, for Christ's sake, with weakness, insults, trouble, persecution, and calamity; for I am strong just when I am weak."

That is prayer.

"Life," said Disraeli, "is too short to be little." André Maurois, who has written about him, describes the man as one who followed the urge of his great spirit through all those difficulties which we have to face, because he would not submit to what he called "little." "Disraeli," concludes Maurois, in his life of the

SPIRITUAL ATHLETICS

Victorian statesman, "was far from being a saint. But perhaps as some old Spirit of Spring, ever vanquished and ever alive, and as a symbol of what can be accomplished in a cold and hostile universe, by a long youthfulness of heart." Prayer is a long youthfulness of the heart—long as eternity is long.

Stand before the fact of the Resurrection. Ponder it until you have made it yours. Such pondering will make you one with him whom we can never understand apart from a spiritual technic for which we can find no better word than *prayer*. Paul saw at last in his own right the mystery of the cross. He saw that the cross was a symbol of the struggle of the soul to keep under its body, knowing that as he reached up to a something finer than his former manhood, he crucified all that was lower in himself.

Like Paul, we are all marked by the stigma of Calvary, and as we endure our crucifixions and lonely Golgothas, we resurrect our true selfhood. Though there is so much we regret and so much of which we are ashamed, we must measure ourselves by memories of those Golgothas, for Christ died to prove that we must die—dying to the flesh that we may resurrect in the spirit. Courage! Follow him, and as you follow, remember that Golgothas include denials, betrayals, and desertions. Meet these experiences with prayer. The power that lifted Jesus from death to life is now operating in us, but we must give that power room to work. How we crowd that power out with our foolish cares, our ignoble pursuits, our thraldom to what Paul describes as "the prince of the air— the spirit which is at present active within those sons of disobedience among whom all of us lived."

PRAYER

Lead us, heavenly Father, by the spirit that is in us through our inheritance—the spirit of strength, courage, and understanding. May we, by the struggle to overcome and guide the mind of the body, develop and guide the mind of the spirit. Strengthened by our Master in the inner spiritual man, may we direct and use the natural man. We would make him our servant and friend whom Thou hast called into being from the dust of the ground. Thou hast blessed him. We would bless him, too, by making him obedient to our deepest purpose, to share with Jesus his abundant life. As our Master used a body, lifting it to the height of his cross, so may we use our bodies, and lift them to the height of our cross. Help us from day to day that we may serve Thee according to Thy will. Amen.

XIII

THE FULNESS OF GOD

Ephesians iii : 19–21

"May you be filled with the entire fulness of God! Now to him who by the action of his power within us can do all things, aye far more than we ever ask or imagine, to him be glory in the church and in Christ Jesus throughout all generations for ever and ever."

Colossians ii : 9–10

"It is in Christ that the entire Fulness of deity has settled bodily, it is in him that you reach your full life, and he is the Head of every angelic Ruler and Power."

As we read these parallel thoughts of Paul about the spiritual body, we are overwhelmed by their implications. How can Christ dwell in our hearts? And how can our mortal nature be filled with the entire fulness of God? For centuries the Church has taught that this fulness

THE FULNESS OF GOD

was centred exclusively in Jesus. Dare we claim this fulness for ourselves? Paul answers: "You must dare, for until you claim the fulness of God, you have not attained the power of the Resurrection."

This leads us back to the original content of the gospel as Paul declared it to his world. He had seen Jesus in bodily form and he never forgot that experience. It led him into the breadth, length, depth, and height of a new life for humanity. We are no longer under the law. We are free from the bondage of death under which our fathers groaned. A greater than Moses has led us forth from servitude. Death is behind us. We are risen with Christ!

Is it any wonder that the Athenian philosophers laughed at him when they heard words like these? Now we understand why he was cast out of the synagogues where he had stoutly made this proclamation of the liberty which Jesus had won for his brethren. Was Paul introducing a thought alien to the teaching of Jesus? He has been accused of that, and it is well to meet this accusation here. Examine the sayings of Jesus as they are treasured in the

Gospels. Begin with the Sermon on the Mount and meditate upon these words: "No one can serve two masters: either he will hate one and love the other, or else he will stand by the one and despise the other—you cannot serve both God and Mammon."

Because he was a Jew, a student of the Old Testament, saturated with its words, Paul could not resist the story of the exodus from Egypt. He thought of Moses as a forerunner of Jesus: as Moses had led his people out of the house of bondage, Jesus had led the human race. But what a difference between these two emancipators! Moses had freed Israel from a tyrant under whose taskmasters the people were forced to make bricks without straw. Jesus had freed the universal Israel from the tyranny of a greater than Pharaoh—death. If we remember how often Jesus spoke against death and how he rebuked those who trembled before its power, we shall begin to understand how loyal Paul was in his teaching, to him who said: "Beware of the leaven of the Pharisees and Sadducees." Paul was reminiscent of that ancient leaven when he wrote:

THE FULNESS OF GOD

"You are free from the old leaven; Christ our paschal lamb has been sacrificed. So let us celebrate our festival, not with any old leaven, not with vice and evil, but with the unleavened bread of innocence and integrity."

Jesus called himself the bread of heaven. There was no ferment of evil or terror in it. That bread was leavened with a new information about man as God's son, eternal in the heavens.

To Paul the crucifixion was inevitable. From the beginning of his ministry, Jesus moved toward that event. It was in his way; he had to meet it. Why? Because as he had said: "I have come that they may have life and have it to the full." Man could not have life in its fulness until Jesus had destroyed the last barrier between God and the soul. That barrier was the fear of death. For this reason, when he wrote his first letter to the Corinthians, Paul posited the cross and the Resurrection as essential to the fulness of the Master's gift to men. Jesus did not die because God was angry with men. He died to sweep away that ancient lie which had deceived men, even as it deceived him who wrote so poignantly: "Shall thy lovingkindness be declared in the grave? or thy faithfulness in destruction?"

From the moment of his conversion, Paul saw that this lie had been pierced by the cross on which the Master died. As his thought matured, Paul turned with awe and wonder toward the true meaning of the cross. Listen to his exultant words about the crucifixion:

"Christ did not send me to baptize but to preach the gospel. And to preach it with no fine rhetoric, lest the cross of Christ should lose its power! Those who are doomed to perish find the story of the cross 'sheer folly,' but it means the power of God for those whom he saves. It is written,

> I will destroy the wisdom of the sages,
> I will confound the insight of the wise.

Sage, scribe, critic of this world, where are they all? Has not God stultified the wisdom of the world? For when the world with all its wisdom failed to know God in his wisdom, God resolved to save believers by the 'sheer folly' of the Christian message. Jews demand miracles and Greeks want wisdom, but our message is Christ the crucified—a stumblingblock to the Jews, 'sheer folly' to the Gentiles, but for those who are called, whether Jews or Greeks, a Christ who is the power of God and the wisdom of God."

"The sheer folly of the Christian message"— that is how Paul described the reactions of people to his words. It is a faithful description of the reaction of our world to this gospel which tells with convincing authority that man may share the entire fulness of God bodily as Jesus shared it. How far have we accepted the Resurrection of our Lord? How we die from day to day, and falter as we leave Egypt behind! Still enslaved by tyrant death, we murmur against our leader, clamoring for the flesh pots.

We are like the slaves whom Moses led, training them in the wilderness for forty years—so the story goes—until they were ready to cross Jordan into the Promised Land. The parallel is not complete without the memory of the fact that Moses failed where Joshua succeeded. Moses could lead the Israelites to the Jordan, but there his work ended. Joshua began where Moses ended. Do we strain the figure when we describe a greater Joshua who has divided the flood to lead us over? Paul must have had this figure in his mind as he carried his gospel through Asia Minor and into Europe. The passage which has been quoted to measure the exultance of Paul about the cross reveals the conflicts that met him as he went on his glorious way, an ambassador of the new life in God which Jesus had brought to light. He faced a world of men doomed to perish in death, as men are still doomed who mock at the cross, calling it sheer folly.

With what shrugging of shoulders does this modern world receive that gospel! And how Paul meets our world with his courageous repetitions: "What I preach does not rest on plausible arguments of the schools. I do not offer you evidences for the survival of the soul. Our faith does not rest on this kind of reasoning. What no eye has ever seen, what no ear has ever heard, what never entered the mind of man, God has prepared all that for those who love Him, and God has revealed it to us by the Spirit, for the Spirit fathoms everything, even the depths of God."

Here we may ask Paul: What do you mean by the Spirit? The word itself has a vague sound. Must we wait for a sudden ecstasy caused by a revelation from God Himself before we can accept this astounding statement? Paul would answer: "No, you must be born again as our Master said. You must have a

THE FULNESS OF GOD

birth from above. That birth is attained only by those who change their centre of consciousness from the physical to the spiritual body. As you enter into that consciousness, you become one with God. Then it is that God speaks to you:

"What human being can understand the thoughts of a man, except the man's own inner spirit? So too no one understands the thoughts of God, except the Spirit of God. Now we have received the Spirit—not the spirit of the world, but the Spirit that comes from God, that we may understand what God bestows upon us. And this is what we discuss, using language taught by no human wisdom but by the Spirit. We interpret what is spiritual in spiritual language. The unspiritual man rejects these truths of the Spirit of God; to him they are 'sheer folly,' he cannot understand them. And the reason is, that they must be read with the spiritual eye. The spiritual man, again, can read the meaning of everything; and yet no one can read what he is. For who ever understood the thoughts of the Lord, so as to give him instruction? No one. Well, our thoughts are Christ's thoughts."

We admit that this reply is not easy to understand, but we do assert that the story of Christianity witnesses to the abounding fulness of eternal life in those who have pondered and finally understood that story. How? By submitting their way to God's way and by following Jesus along the path which he travelled from the garden of Gethsemane to Calvary. If we refuse to follow that path, we must be content with the tyranny of death. But if we would shake off that tyranny, we must be obedient to him who wrote: "Fight in the good fight of the faith, secure that life eternal."

Man may be filled with the entire fulness of God, the fulness of the Deity that settled bodily in Christ. We know that fulness. It is the fulness of life—life that conquered death. The gospel of Jesus as Paul preached it offers us present victory over death.

PRAYER

Thou who art the God and Father of us all, in whom we live, move, and have our being, hast called us from death to life through Jesus our Master. To Thee we bow in adoration. We cannot offer Thee words to describe the thoughts of our hearts that struggle in vain with speech, but we can offer ourselves to Thee—ourselves in the unity of the natural and spiritual man.

THE FULNESS OF GOD

Help us by the grace of Jesus to crucify the flesh with its cravings that war against the freedom of our true selves. We do not ask to enter the Promised Land without the cleaving of Jordan and the peril of its passing. We are ready to begin the new life, ready to be trained to possess it, for we know that the trivial round and the common task of every day will provide us with tests of our endurance and strength. May we overcome sin in the flesh, and lay hold on that eternal life which Jesus has offered, and still offers, for us all. Strengthened by him in our souls, may we go on undismayed by the clamor of those who call for the flesh pots of Egypt, as we hear him say, "Follow me!" Amen.

XIV

CLOTHED WITH IMMORTALITY

Romans viii : 1–11

"There is no doom now for those who are in Christ Jesus; the law of the Spirit brings the life which is in Christ Jesus, and that law has set me free from the law of sin and death. For God has done what the Law, weakened here by the flesh, could not do; by sending his own Son in the guise of sinful flesh, to deal with sin, he condemned sin in the flesh, in order to secure the fulfilment of the Law's requirements in our lives, as we live and move not by the flesh, but by the Spirit.

*For those who follow the flesh have their interests in
    the flesh,
and those who follow the Spirit have their interests
    in the Spirit.
The interests of the flesh meant death,
the interests of the Spirit meant life and peace.*

For the interests of the flesh are hostile to God; they do not yield to the law of God (indeed they cannot). Those who are in the flesh cannot satisfy God. But you are not in the flesh, you are in the Spirit, since the Spirit of God dwells within you. Anyone who does not possess the Spirit of Christ does not belong to Him. On the other hand, if Christ is within you, though the body is a dead thing owing to Adam's sin, the spirit is living as the result of righteousness. And if the Spirit of Him who raised Jesus from the dead dwells within you, then He who raised Christ from the dead will also make your mortal bodies live by his indwelling Spirit in your lives."

CAN we experience the historical fact of the Resurrection now? Can we build that fact into our lives?

Many who accept the Resurrection of Jesus base on it their faith in immortality. Some of us were taught that the doctrine of immortality without the resurrection of the physical body is a mutilation of the Christian faith; that after death the disembodied soul rests in an intermediate state, Paradise, until the last day when, at the coming of Christ, soul and body shall be

HIS GLORIOUS BODY

reunited. This doctrine persists in the words of interment used in the burial service:

"Unto Almighty God we commend the soul of our brother departed, and we commit his body to the ground; earth to earth, ashes to ashes, dust to dust; in sure and certain hope of the Resurrection unto eternal life, through our Lord Jesus Christ; at whose coming in glorious majesty to judge the world, the earth and the sea shall give up their dead; and the corruptible bodies of those who sleep in him shall be changed, and made like unto his own glorious body; according to the mighty working whereby he is able to subdue all things unto himself."

Then there is another view of the Resurrection which teaches that, as the soul departs, it clothes itself with a spiritual counterpart already nucleated in the former body. This would explain the true Resurrection, accounting for the manifestations of Jesus after his death: he did not appear to his disciples in the body which was crucified, but in an astral or etheric form which he drew from the crucified body when it died on the cross.

If either of these interpretations of the resurrected life is true, then our argument is invalid. From our study of Paul's letters, we have

CLOTHED WITH IMMORTALITY

derived that the soul has two bodies, one carnal, the other spiritual, and that death is not necessary to the release of the spiritual body. All this is in the teaching of the New Testament. Jesus' death and Resurrection were demonstrations of man's deathlessness. But how hard it is for us to apply this to ourselves who are confronted by the inevitable question: How can we resurrect now?

We find the answer in Paul's letters. His ethics are not other-worldly. His vision of the righteous man is not millenarian. Though some of his words seem to justify the position of those who quote him to prove their belief in post-mortem immortality, the key-note of his thought is given in the phrase: "That I may know him, and the power of his resurrection." According to Paul, when the soul leaves its flesh body, it is not clothed with the spiritual body as with a new garment. That spiritual body is the soul's true inheritance, with which it goes forth as of old along the path of initiation. If we could grasp this, how our thinking toward our present life would change!

We are already clothed with immortality.

HIS GLORIOUS BODY

The wedding garment is already ours, and it is our shame if, when the Master comes, he finds us without that garment. By living to the flesh body, we sit down at the supper of our Lord without that wedding garment. "May Christ dwell in your hearts as you have faith." What Christ? Paul answers: "The now-living Christ, and the continuous communion and relationship of your life with the life of him who has conquered death."

"As you have faith!" Faith is a word that describes a man's knowledge of a power that works. Faith is not blind. Faith is a certainty. Christian faith is not speculative but experimental. A Christian is one who knows Jesus, the resurrected Master. However he may have been helped by books—books like the New Testament and its derivatives—he has won his knowledge by applying to himself in daily living the facts of the Resurrection.

We have a great inheritance, and we are as one might be who has suddenly acquired, through the death of a friend, an unexpected fortune. How a life of poverty would at first stagger at the thought, "I am no longer poor.

CLOTHED WITH IMMORTALITY

I am released from the constraint of little economies. I am free to do good, to help those whom I love!" That is how Paul would have us react to the gift of our Master. He is definite and clear in his thinking about the freedom of the new life which he has found. With what joy he writes:

> "There is no doom now for those who are in Christ Jesus; the law of the Spirit brings the life which is in Christ Jesus, and that law has set me free from the law of sin and death. . . . And if the Spirit of Him who raised Jesus from the dead dwells within you, then He who raised Christ from the dead will also make your mortal bodies live by his indwelling Spirit in your lives.
>
> "Well, then, my brothers, we owe a duty—but it is not to the flesh! If you live by the flesh, you are on the road to death; but if by the Spirit you put the actions of the body to death, you will live."

This eighth chapter of the Epistle to the Romans is our Magna Carta and ought to be committed to memory and repeated as often as we are tempted to return to our old poverty, denying by a slavish dread the fathomless wealth of Christ.

All this is in the gospel of the Resurrection which Paul preached with such increasing power. This power dwells in our hearts through our experience of its effect upon our lives as we put it to the test. The tests are described in a phrase: "May you be so fixed and founded in love." Love is the narrow gate that leads into the boundless life of the resurrection. As we love, we resurrect, overcoming the carnal body with all its discordant voices. Do you know the terror of the African jungle at night? When the sun sets, comes the roar of the lion, the snarl of the tiger, the laughter of the hyena, the chatter of the monkey, the hiss of the serpent, the wail of the helpless under the fangs or in the coils of hideous death. In this we have a parable of the former man from whom there is no escape until we have overcome him by the power of that other man who is eternal in the heavens.

We must work out our own salvation against the fear of the jungle. Make no compromise with that terror, which the Master met and conquered for us all. Accept his gift. It is fully ours. Take it without reservation, for we are now no longer after the flesh but after the spirit. We are in eternal life.

That is what Paul would say to us now; and he would add:

> "I am certain neither death nor life, neither angels nor principalities, neither the present nor the future, no powers of the Height or of the Depth, nor anything else in all creation will be able to part us from God's love in Christ Jesus our Lord."

PRAYER

Indwelling Spirit of our God, strengthen our faith against the despondency and doubt of the natural man. Help us to measure the breadth, length, depth, and height of the love of him who has given us eternal life through his Resurrection. We acknowledge our imperfections and are sore distressed by our disloyalties to the lordship of our souls. May we walk with Jesus along the path of that life which overcame death. As he rebuked the winds and the sea, may we rebuke the snarl, the chatter, the hiss, and the cry of that shadowed and unhappy life out of which we have come into the freedom of the sons of God. With this freedom, may we be made strong to release our brothers by the power of his Resurrection. Amen.

XV

ONE BODY AND ONE SPIRIT

Ephesians iv : 1–6

"As the Lord's prisoner, then, I beg of you to live a life worthy of your calling, with perfect modesty and gentleness, showing forbearance to one another patiently, zealous in love to preserve the unity of the Spirit by binding peace upon yourselves. For there is one Body and one Spirit—as you were called for the one hope that belongs to your call—one Lord, one faith, one baptism, one God and Father of all, who is over us all, who pervades us all, who is within us all."

Paul was in prison when he wrote these words. As he looked at the walls of his dungeon, he remembered that other dungeon from which Jesus had released him. That dungeon was death. He had been born into it. From a little child the thought of dying had been thrust into him by those who loved him best, his father and

ONE BODY AND ONE SPIRIT

his mother. With all its beauty, their religion was marred by a terror of death. As we have already seen, though there are glimpses of immortality in the Old Testament, by comparison with the gospel of the Resurrection it offers only a few crumbs of hope to the sorrowing.

This explains Paul's enthusiasm about the Resurrection. The living Jesus had forever released him from the terrors of death. Paul was an educated man, conversant with the speculations of philosophers, poets, and religious teachers about immortality. At best, they were vague and unconvincing. If he had examined either Buddha or Plato—and there is no reason to doubt that he had—he gathered little from them. He was not converted to the Paul of these letters by either of these masters. He was changed from despair to joy and certainty on the Damascus road. Whatever Buddha or Plato meant by the reincarnation of the soul, they did not mean what Paul found in Jesus. New information about the soul and its place in eternity throbs through every word Paul wrote after that experience.

In the course of time Paul was imprisoned by

Cæsar. In the Acts of the Apostles there is a convincing bit of autobiography which explains why Cæsar put Paul in a dungeon. Waiting at Cæsarea to be tried by Felix, Paul at last stood before his judge. His accusers were the high priest Annas, together with a few elders, possibly members of the Sanhedrin, and a lawyer called Tertullus, who apologized for bothering Felix with such unimportant matters, and added:

" 'The fact is, we have found this man is a perfect pest; he stirs up sedition among the Jews all over the world and he is a ringleader of the Nazarene sect. He actually tried to desecrate the temple, but we got hold of him. Examine him for yourself and you will be able to find out about all these charges of ours against him.' "

"A perfect pest"—what a familiar sound! Thus many would describe Paul to-day. Socrates was called a perfect pest by his accusers in Athens for talking so much about the immortality of the soul. People who are busied with the affairs of the flesh are impatient with discussions which intrude upon business and interfere with social duties. How can one regulate the politics of the world with the troubling

ONE BODY AND ONE SPIRIT

thought of a possibly different kind of world, a world of spirit where love is law and God is all in all?

Such was the mood of those who accused Paul in the court of Felix, who, with a casual nod, permitted the prisoner before him to defend himself. This defense rested upon Paul's experience of the new life in Jesus: "It is for the resurrection of the dead that I am on my trial to-day before you." Felix gave no indication of any interest in this astounding doctrine, though he seems to have been affected, for, several days after the trial, he summoned Paul for a private interview in the presence of his wife, Drusilla. Was it Drusilla who managed that interview? Anyway, Felix heard Paul's story. He appears to have been interested in the problem of immortality, but he was evidently not prepared to apply the Resurrection to himself. For when Paul talked about morality, self-mastery, and the future judgment, Felix began to evade the issue. He was uneasy. The gospel of the Resurrection always makes the carnal man uneasy. The flesh man is rebellious and unwilling to yield to the spirit man, for the power of the Resurrection is gained by the discipline of the body.

Felix concluded the interview by dismissing Paul with a curt: "You may go for the present. When I can find a moment I will send for you." According to the story, he did send frequently for his prisoner and talked with him. But it ended in talk. Felix lost his opportunity. So for two years Paul remained in Cæsarea under custody.

Felix was succeeded by Porcius Festus, who in time ordered Paul to appear before the tribunal. Festus was an opportunist and tried to use Paul for political reasons. Paul, seeing through this scheme, stood his ground by appealing to Cæsar, and took the matter of his trial out of Festus' hands. A few days after this appeal, Festus entertained king Agrippa and his wife Bernice, and in the course of their talking about many things, Festus said:

"There is a man who was left in prison by Felix. When I was at Jerusalem, the high priests and elders of the Jews informed me about him and demanded his condemnation: I told them Romans were not in the habit of giving up any man until the accused met the accusers face to face and had a chance of de-

ONE BODY AND ONE SPIRIT

fending himself against the impeachment. Well, the day after they came here along with me, I took my seat on the tribunal without any loss of time. I ordered the man to be brought in, but when his accusers stood up they did not charge him with any of the crimes that I had expected. The questions at issue referred to their own religion and to a certain Jesus who had died. Paul said he was alive. As I felt at a loss about the method of inquiry into such topics, I asked if he would go to Jerusalem and be tried there on these charges. But Paul entered an appeal for his case to be reserved for the decision of the emperor; so I ordered him to be detained till I could remit him to Cæsar."

How modern all this sounds! So the rulers of our world would handle the case if it were brought before them. They, too, would feel "at a loss about the method of inquiry into such topics" as the crucified and risen Jesus. Festus, Agrippa, and Bernice, can you escape the cross and the Resurrection? What will you do with this Jesus called Christ, who appeared to Paul and convinced him by many infallible proofs of the reality of our eternal and spiritual manhood?

Paul must have been thinking of those years at Cæsarea, lamenting over Felix, hoping for Drusilla and wondering how he could reach

HIS GLORIOUS BODY

people like Agrippa and Bernice. In spite of their indifference, they had been affected by something in Paul which set him apart from all other men. As we read of the entertainment which Festus gave in honor of Agrippa and Bernice in the judgment hall with high pomp of military commanders and prominent citizens of Cæsarea, we are compelled to admit that the preaching of the crucified and risen Lord was not confined to slaves and obscure peasants. That charge, which has often been made, is without any historical foundation. Cæsarea was a port, one of the maritime gateways that opened between Europe and Asia, and here in the great hall of judgment, before the representatives of Cæsar, emperor of the world, Paul told his story. Whoever reported that episode must have been present, for this noble defense of the gospel is one of the most inspired, clear, and reasoned utterances which the New Testament records. It is stamped with the personality of the man Paul, and closes with a question which still challenges the world:

"Why should you consider it incredible that God raises the dead, that the Christ is capable of suffering, and that he should be the first to rise from the dead and bring the message of life to the People and to the Gentiles?"

This leads us back to the story of Paul imprisoned by Cæsar and thinking, as he would, of that mental dungeon whose door Jesus the Master had opened for him that he might go forth into everlasting life. It was then that he added these words to his Ephesian letter: "As the Lord's prisoner, then, I beg of you to live a life worthy of your calling."

What calling? In the second letter attributed by tradition to Peter, there is an answer to this question:

"Inasmuch as his power divine has bestowed on us every requisite for life and piety by the knowledge of him who called us to his own glory and excellence—bestowing on us thereby promises precious and supreme, that by means of them you may escape the corruption produced within the world by lust, and participate in the divine nature—for this very reason, do you contrive to make it your whole concern to furnish your faith with resolution, resolution with intelligence, intelligence with self-control, self-control with stedfastness, stedfastness with piety, piety with brotherliness, brotherliness with Christian love. . . . So be the more eager, brothers, to ratify your calling and election, for as you practise these qualities you will never make a slip; you will thus be richly furnished with the right of entry into the eternal realm of our Lord and saviour Jesus Christ."

If what Paul declared in his letters is true; if Jesus by the Resurrection has demonstrated our divinity, then we are called to attain all that he has revealed in himself. We are called to the attainment of the character of Jesus. We are called to live eternally with ourselves as sons of the living God. We are called to live worthily of the race on which we are now entered, called to run it with patience. With patience—we must remember that. "Be patient first with yourself," Paul would say. "Be patient with your weakness. Do not be discouraged by the aching hands and the bleeding feet and the dimming eyes. You are now an athlete of God. Develop your spiritual muscle by a daily routine of exercise. Practise your divinity."

If we say to him, "How can we practise our divinity?" Paul will answer what he wrote to the Ephesians:

"'Wake up, O sleeper, and rise from the dead;
so Christ will shine upon you.'
"Be strictly careful then about the life you lead;

ONE BODY AND ONE SPIRIT

act like sensible men, not like thoughtless; make the very most of your time, for these are evil days. So do not be senseless, but understand what is the Lord's will. . . . Be strong in the Lord and in the strength of his might; put on God's armour so as to be able to stand against the stratagems of the devil. For we have to struggle, not with blood and flesh but with the angelic Rulers, the angelic Authorities, the potentates of the dark present, the spirit-forces of evil in the heavenly sphere. . . . Hold your ground."

A prisoner of Jesus under the will of Cæsar, Paul's words must have reached the throne under whose majesty he now languished in darkness. He addressed that throne, the symbol of the ancient tyranny of death, with words which we must ultimately heed:

"There is one Body and one Spirit—as you were called for the one hope that belongs to your call—one Lord, one faith, one baptism, one God and Father of all, who is over us all, who pervades us all, who is within us all."

PRAYER

We who are prisoners of Christ, address Thee, dear Father, in one hope of our eternal calling. May we live worthily of that calling, making it sure by obedience to the life of perfect modesty and gentleness. Thou art the God and Father of Jesus and of those for whom he died.

Deepen our faith and purify us by the blood of him who has baptized us from death to life, that we may know Thee as sons in the fellowship of our Master.   Amen.

XVI

THE GLORY OF MAN'S INHERITANCE

Ephesians iv : 17–32

"Now in the Lord I insist and protest that you must give up living like pagans; for their purposes are futile, their intelligence is darkened, they are estranged from the life of God by the ignorance which their dulness of heart has produced in them—men who have recklessly abandoned themselves to sensuality, with a lust for the business of impurity in every shape and form. That is not how you have understood the meaning of Christ (for it is Christ whom you have been taught, it is in Christ that you have been instructed—the real Christ who is in Jesus); you must lay aside the old nature which belonged to your former course of life, that nature which crumbles to ruin under the passions of moral deceit, and be renewed in the spirit of your mind, putting on the new nature, that divine pattern which has been created in the upright and pious character of the Truth.

HIS GLORIOUS BODY

...ide falsehood, then, let each tell his ...r the truth, for we are members one of ...nother. Be angry but do not sin; never let the sun set upon your exasperation, give the devil no chance. Let the thief steal no more; rather let him work and put his hands to an honest task, so as to have something to contribute to the needy. Let no bad word pass your lips, but only such speech as is good for edification, as occasion may require, words that are gracious and a means of grace to those who hear them. And do not vex God's holy Spirit, by whom you have been sealed for the day of redemption. Drop all bitter feeling and passion and anger and clamoring and insults, together with all malice; be kind to each other, be tender-hearted, be generous to each other as God has been generous to you in Christ. Copy God, then, as his beloved children, and lead lives of love, just as Christ loved you and gave himself up for you to be a fragrant offering and sacrifice to God."

THERE is one body. It is the body of the Resurrection in which Jesus appeared to his disciples after his death. Paul saw that body,

THE GLORY OF MAN'S INHERITANCE

talked with it, and was converted by it. That conversion was not an emotional change. He called it a mental renewal, for Paul was accustomed by his training to subject all experience to his reason. He described Christian discipleship as " a reasonable service." There was more than feeling in that service; it was animated by careful thinking.

We have come to see that the letters of Paul, apart from their personal quality, are charged with a vital philosophy based upon new information concerning the destiny of man. While it is true that Paul described two bodies—a natural and a spiritual—which the soul uses in its progress toward the fulness of eternal life, he regarded the flesh vehicle as only temporary. The other is eternal. Our true body is spiritual; it is identical with the body of the Resurrection.

These thoughts are preliminary to an understanding of the portion of the Ephesian letter which is now before us. We have already discussed the origin of Paul's ethics and have found that they are not moral as morality is ordinarily understood. Morals, according to

Paul, are methods of developing and directing the activities of the spiritual body.

When Nicodemus came to Jesus and said: "Rabbi, we know you have come from God to teach us, for no one could perform these Signs of yours unless God were with him," Jesus replied: "Truly, truly I tell you, no one can see God's Realm unless he is born from above." Nicodemus was disturbed by this reply and asked: "How can a man be born when he is old? Can he enter his mother's womb over again and be born?" Jesus answered: "Truly, truly I tell you, unless one is born of water and the Spirit, he cannot enter God's Realm. What is born of the flesh is flesh: what is born of the Spirit is spirit."

If you compare the Master's words with Paul's teaching, you will see that they bear upon the ethical system of that apostle. Nicodemus acknowledged that Jesus revealed a power which set him apart from all other men. Paul asserted that this was the power of the Resurrection. He was as eager as Nicodemus to manifest this power in himself, but, unlike Nicodemus, he believed that he could do what Jesus

THE GLORY OF MAN'S INHERITANCE

did by practising the Master's way of living.

Here is a fact which is often forgotten by those who study Paul's letters, accepting them as witnesses to the historical Resurrection of our Lord: Paul preached as he wrote. This was his doctrine: "We are children of God; and if children, heirs as well, heirs of God, heirs along with Christ—for we share his sufferings in order to share his glory."

What were those sufferings? Scientific disciplines of training the spiritual body to share with Jesus the glory of man's inheritance. "Present suffering," he added, "is a mere nothing compared to the glory that we are to have revealed."

Because there is one true body which we inherit from God together with the Master, whose life was a demonstration of its eternal reality, Paul argued that the sins of the flesh were interferences with the disciplines necessary to the training of our present spiritual body. That is why he wrote:

"You must lay aside the old nature which belonged to your former course of life, that nature which crumbles to ruin under the passions of moral

HIS GLORIOUS BODY

deceit, and be renewed in the spirit of your mind, putting on the new nature, that divine pattern which has been created in the upright and pious character of the Truth. Lay aside falsehood, then, let each tell his neighbor the truth, for we are members one of another."

Here we have a description of the unity of the spiritual body. Through that body we are one with the Master, whose cross is an indication of the method by which he was able to demonstrate in the flesh the dominion of the spiritual body. But this dominion implies a unity of body and soul, for, at best, bodies are vehicles of the soul, and as wonderful as the spiritual body is, it is only a servant under the lordship of God's son. This son is the soul, to whom God gave bodies as it needed them, bodies to be conformed to the soul as it increased in wisdom and in stature, and in favor with God and man.

Now we are ready for the glad, brave struggle of the Christian life. We are no longer disturbed by the physical world to which we seem to belong. That world is in itself one of our bodies. We are identified with it, but we must be superior to it. "In the world you have trouble, but courage! I have conquered the

THE GLORY OF MAN'S INHERITANCE

world." But that is not enough for the Christian. He seeks, under the leadership of Jesus, to overcome the world in his own right as a son of God. And he who seeks to win such a victory will do well to submit to the disciplines which Paul has so carefully elaborated and described. These disciplines are in the path where we stand together now. We must not shrink from them if we would gain the power of the Resurrection. Let us move onward in the joyous ascent of the soul along the path of attainment.

Do you ask for a scientific proof of immortality? Find the answer in its practice. That careless word, that angry thought, that covered arrogance, that overshadowing despair, that wounding sorrow and useless worry, are among your disciplines. As you overcome, you will know the unity of your body and soul with him who said: "He who possesses my commands and obeys them is he who loves me, and he who loves me will be loved by my Father, and I will love him and appear to him." In this saying of the Master are the roots of Paul's ethics. Loving Jesus is more than an ardent af-

HIS GLORIOUS BODY

fection for a beautiful life. It is a clear and studied appraisal of its values, privileges, and unrestricted freedom.

What are some of these values? An understanding of the significance of what we call, for want of a better word, our personality. This personality is compounded of the members which constitute our visible body. This body is a mask, important to the part which we play in the drama of eternity. Make the most of that body. Guard its health and train it to an increasing capacity to serve among many brethren. Jesus made his flesh body the means of the world's redemption. He submitted to the lash, the nails, and the thorns. Shall we not also accept these tests? Do not run away from them, or rail against environment. In that state of life to which we have been called, we must do our duty as Jesus did.

What are some of the privileges? We look back to the Master in the days of his physical embodiment for our answer. He healed the sick, gave sight to the blind, and filled the hearts of those who loved him with a peace which passed all understanding. If we would possess and use

THE GLORY OF MAN'S INHERITANCE

our spiritual body now, we must let its radiance shine before men as he did. The story that is told of Peter may be told of us. So faithfully had he followed the way of his Master that "invalids were actually carried into the streets and laid on beds and mattresses, so that, when Peter passed, his shadow at any rate might fall on one or other of them."

Think of the freedom of the resurrected life! What kind of freedom? As we raise this question, we think of old anxieties which tormented us before our lives were hid with Christ in God. How we worried over the question of the psalmist: "Shall thy lovingkindness be declared in the grave?" To the man who has entered upon the inheritance of his spiritual body, death has no terror because it no longer exists. He knows that there are no dead except those who are still living in their lower vehicles, regardless of that spiritual body which is one with the risen body of the Master. However imperfectly such a man demonstrates the dominion of the higher over the lower body, he knows that, as that dominion grows, his information about those who have gone before him will become clearer. So he

HIS GLORIOUS BODY

is content to practise the athletics of his soul. If he is asked by the doubter, "How can you say there are no dead when the world is a sepulchre to which at every moment a multitude is carried and to which you in your time will also be carried?" he will answer: "Though this body which you see is growing old and though at last it dies, I know that my Redeemer lives and that in the true body I shall see God."

We are under no illusion about the Resurrection. Though thousands of years must pass before humanity accepts and practises the Resurrection in its power, the day will dawn when man will prove as a son of God: "I have power over my body; I have power to lay it down and also power to take it up again."

PRAYER

Dear Master, who taught us that only the pure in heart can see God, cleanse our hearts by the inspiration of the Holy Spirit that we may lay aside the old nature which belonged to our former course of life, the nature of the carnal body crumbling into ruin under the passions of moral deceit.

Clothe us, by the renewing of our minds, with the divine pattern which is revealed in thee. Teach us to be kind and tender-hearted to one another; and as thou didst copy God, so may we, thy brethren and His beloved children, give ourselves up to Him, for we have been sealed by thy cross for the day of redemption. Amen.

XVII

THE WITNESS OF WORDS

Ephesians v : 3–14

"Never let any sexual vice or impurity or lust be so much as mentioned by you—that is the proper course for saints to take; no, nor indecent, silly, or scurrilous talk—all that is improper. Rather, voice your thanks to God. Be sure of this, that no one guilty of sexual vice or impurity or lust (that is, an idolator) possesses any inheritance in the realm of Christ and God. Let no one deceive you with specious arguments; these are the vices that bring down God's anger on the sons of disobedience. So avoid the company of such men. For while once upon a time you were darkness, now in the Lord you are light; lead the life of those who are children of the light (for the fruit of light consists in all that is good and right and true), verifying what pleases the Lord. Have nothing to do with the fruitless enterprises of the darkness; rather expose them. One is indeed ashamed

even to speak about what such men do in secret; still, whatever the light exposes becomes illuminated—for anything that is illuminated turns into light."

These words were written in one of the most corrupt periods of the human race. They were written by a man who was never a hypocrite. Sincerity tempered all his faults, and his faults, by his own confession, were many. He wrote with authority about the social evils of the world to which he belonged. This world was awaking to the sound of a new message, which was nowhere being uttered with such convincing power as by the man Paul. People were restless and unhappy about their social iniquities, and many were shrinking in horror from the impudent parading of vice.

The moral corruption of the world when Paul was a prisoner at Rome is one of the facts of history and need not here be described. Glimpses of that corruption are given in Paul's letters. It is a tragic story that belongs to the beginning of the gospel of Jesus as it was preached by his disciples. But the story helps us to understand the eagerness with which many listened to what the disciples had to say about a new kind of life. No wonder that the words *salvation, redemption, atonement,* recur with an almost monotonous frequency in the preaching of the earliest followers of the Master. These men had no illusions about the world. It was in a perilous state, and they believed that civilization could be saved by their preaching. Whatever theories of ultimate damnation may have entered into that preaching, these theories were derived from an experience with an order of society which was already convincingly damned by its results.

So, when Paul wrote his Ephesian letter, he had before him a social disorder which could not be ignored by one who had found a new life in Jesus. As we have seen, Paul's ethics were related to that experience. He believed that the spiritual body could be attained as man submitted to the disciplines or exercises of initiation. To be initiated into the possession of the spiritual body, the candidate or disciple must renounce the impulses and habits of the carnal body. "If," he said, "you would attain the possession

THE WITNESS OF WORDS

of your spiritual body, exercise self-control—not that there is anything evil in the carnal body. Its impulses are native to it, but if you obey them, you become its prisoner. Do you ask me, How can I escape from that prison? I answer: Practise your spirituality."

Then follows this advice, which has never been surpassed by any subsequent code of ethics: "Never let any sexual vice or impurity or lust be so much as mentioned by you—that is the proper course for saints to take."

What did Paul mean by *saints*? We have been accustomed to thinking about saints as solitary, emaciated, abnormal people, who for the inheritance of heaven have given up the normal use of this world. We are hardly to be blamed for thinking of saints as pathological specimens. Centuries of pious stories about holy men and women have succeeded in building such a wall of legend about them that we have come to regard the saints either as occasional messengers from God to an evil world or as spectacular freaks with whom we have nothing to do.

Paul described a saint as one who had responded to the call of the Resurrection, who had

HIS GLORIOUS BODY

broken the door of death by a thrust of the Master's cross—the thrust of sacrifice or self-discipline. The heaven of a saint is the possession of his spiritual body while he still abides in that lower vehicle, the flesh body. So the proper course for saints—disciples who have accepted the new life in Jesus—is to set aside whatever interferes with the freedom of that new life. No one knew better than Paul what that freedom was.

How humble he was in the acknowledgment of his faults. How he has described them! He did not scruple to recapture the days when he was under the dominion of the flesh body. In writing to the disciples at Rome, he dramatized his former life with such vividness of detail that, as we read his words, they sound as though he were still under the dominion of the carnal man:

"I am a creature of the flesh, in the thraldom of sin. I cannot understand my own actions; I do not act as I want to act; on the contrary, I do what I detest. . . . For in me (that is, in my flesh) no good dwells, I know; the wish is there, but not the power of doing what is right. I cannot be good as I want to be, and I do wrong against my wishes. Well, if I act against my wishes, it is not I who do the deed but sin that dwells within me."

THE WITNESS OF WORDS

When Paul wrote this little drama of his former life, he was not forgetful of the new life which he shared with Jesus. But he was seeking to convince men of the futility of trying to live under the dominion of the carnal mind and at the same time claiming to be in the way of inheriting the spiritual mind. He described these inconsistent ones as miserable wretches imprisoned in a body of death. "Escape from your prison by the power of the cross," he cried, "and crucify the old self!"

There is a proper course for saints to take, and it begins with the control of the tongue. "Let everyone," wrote the author of the Epistle of James, "be quick to listen, slow to talk. . . . Whoever avoids slips of speech is a perfect man; he can bridle the whole of the body as well as the tongue."

The writer of this letter knew Paul or was familiar with his teaching. Together they shared the power of the Resurrection. They were practising that power. They knew by experience that careless speech led one back from a new to an old habit, the habit of the carnal body.

HIS GLORIOUS BODY

Here is the statement of a new technic of life. Christianity is that technic. We call it *Christianity* because it derives from Jesus, who is called *Christ* because he mastered the technic of the Resurrection. We love his name *Jesus* because he built up this technic for us as well as for himself. Jesus resurrected into the new life on the hill of the Transfiguration. It was this resurrection or attainment that Christed him, and until we see that the word *Christ* describes this attainment, we shall never, in the present state to which we belong, inherit his abundant manhood. Somewhere along the path he submitted to the tests, and his utterances are reminiscent of them: "He who is not with me is against me, and he who does not gather with me scatters. I tell you therefore, men will be forgiven any sin and blasphemy, but they will not be forgiven for blaspheming the Spirit. Whoever says a word against the Son of Man will be forgiven, but whoever speaks against the holy Spirit will never be forgiven, neither in this world nor in the world to come."

If this be true, then the tongue can doom a man to the peril of many embodiments, until

THE WITNESS OF WORDS

he has acquired strength to set himself free from that damnation. Every word that describes our infidelity to the indwelling spirit of God, the soul, made in His image and likeness, is blasphemy against the holy Ghost.

Here we are on the border of that outer darkness which theologians have described as the "unforgivable sin." Of course, no sin can be unforgivable, but we may set up conditions so terrible in their consequences that a prolonged imprisonment of the soul in matter may result. We do not presume to push this too far; it is wise at this point to be humble with Browning:

> "Else I avert my face, nor follow him
> Into that sad obscure sequestered state
> Where God unmakes but to remake the soul
> He else made first in vain; which must not be."

But we have not carried this thought to its conclusion. For the Master added: "Either make the tree good and its fruit good, or make the tree rotten and its fruit rotten; for the tree is known by its fruit. You brood of vipers, how can you speak good when you are evil? For the mouth utters what the heart is full of. The good

HIS GLORIOUS BODY

man brings good out of his good store, and the evil man brings evil out of his store of evil. I tell you, men will have to account on the day of judgment for every light word they utter; for by your words you will be acquitted, and by your words you will be condemned."

Behind this statement of our Lord is the story of his own initiation and attainment. He became what he was by overcoming as we must overcome. It was said of Jesus by those who heard him, "Never man spake like this man." Did the Master come to this supremacy of speech in a moment? "No," answers Luke; "he increased in wisdom and in stature, and in favor with God and man."

If, then, we would inherit everlasting life, which is another way of describing the resurrection body, we must begin by training the tongue to represent, not our physical, but our spiritual manhood. One of the symptoms of the decadent civilization which Paul and his companions were seeking to rescue was the shallow tittle-tattle of society in all its ramifications. He described this social iniquity as "indecent, silly, and scurrilous talk."

THE WITNESS OF WORDS

Men who are set toward nobility of living have no time in their conversation for gossip about those things which represent the former life lived while they were under the dominion of death. It is characteristic of those who have faced and endured prolonged danger that they seldom refer to it. After the war, we soon found that the men who returned were reticent about its tragic happenings.

"Once upon a time," said Paul, "you were darkness, now in the Lord you are light; lead the life of those who are children of the light (for the fruit of light consists in all that is good and right and true), verifying what pleases the Lord. Have nothing to do with the fruitless enterprises of the darkness; rather expose them. One is indeed ashamed even to speak about what such men do in secret; still, whatever the light exposes becomes illuminated—for anything that is illuminated turns into light."

Here is a saying hard to understand. We can believe that trivial talk of any kind is a disloyalty to the higher body, but we surely cannot believe that it is our business to discuss the evil lives of other people in order to expose

[167]

them. Paul did not mean that. He meant that, as we live in the light of the Resurrection, we see how futile idle words are. We know that he meant this, for we have heard him say: "When I was a child, I talked like a child, I thought like a child, I argued like a child; now that I am a man, I am done with childish ways."

This is the light that shows us the emptiness of words which are not regulated by the new consciousness. As a writer is careful of his style, a gentleman of his manners, so will a Christian control his tongue, saying nothing that would insult or misrepresent the new life which he has found in God through his resurrected Lord.

We give reality to things by our words. We have turned our faces toward the abundant life of the Resurrection. We no longer walk in darkness. We are no more under the dominion of the physical world. Why then give reality to that darkness and that world? Jesus' way is best: "Enter into the consciousness of your divine manhood and shut the door against the lower world. Talk with your Father in that secret place, and He will reward you openly. Men will know that you are risen with me by your conversation. Freely you have received, freely give."

PRAYER

O eternal Word, incarnate, living in our midst, grant to us thy disciples the beauty of truth upon our tongue. We who have turned our faces toward the abundant life of thy Resurrection would preach that gospel to the ends of the earth. May the words of our mouth and the meditations of our heart always be acceptable unto thee. Confirm our words with the following signs of discipleship, that we may heal the sick, give sight to the blind, hearing to the deaf, speech to the dumb, and life to the dead.

Lord, to whom shall we go, for thou hast the words of eternal life? Write them on our hearts and inspire them as they fall from our lips, that we may be witnesses among men of the appeal of thy cross and the challenge of thy Resurrection. Amen.

XVIII

THE CHURCH OF GOD

Ephesians v : 32–vi : 9

"This is a profound symbol, I mean as regards Christ and the church. However, let every man of you love his wife as himself, and let the wife reverence her husband. Children, obey your parents in the Lord, for this is right; honour your father and mother (it is the first command with a promise), that it may be well with you and that you may live long on earth. As for you fathers, do not exasperate your children, but bring them up in the discipline and on the admonitions of the Lord.

"Servants, be obedient to those who are your masters here below with reverence and trembling, with singleness of heart as to Christ himself; instead of merely working when their eye is on you, like those who court human favour, do God's will from the heart like servants of Christ, by rendering service with good-will as to the Lord and Master, not to men. Be sure that everyone, slave or free, will be paid back by

the Lord and Master for the good he has done. And as for you masters, act by your servants in the same way, and stop threatening them; be sure that they and you have a Lord and Master in heaven, and there is no partiality about him."

To understand these words, we must go back to the days of the Roman Empire when this letter was written. Christianity has been described as a religion of other-worldliness. It was not so regarded by the disciples of the first century. To them it was practical, bearing upon the little problems of domestic life. That is why the gospel made such universal appeal wherever it was preached. It satisfied the lovers, as it challenged them to consecrate themselves to the disciplines without which a home was like a house builded on the sand. The acceptance of Jesus as the Master of a new way of living united the believers into one great family. This family was a spiritual house, builded of living stones—individual families cemented together by loyalty to the principles of the resurrected life.

HIS GLORIOUS BODY

This describes the origin of the word *church*. Any family was an *ecclesia*. The word at first meant no more than a united household consecrated to the discipline of Jesus. Instances of this use of the word *church* as applied to the home abound in Paul's letters:

"The household of Stephanas, you know, was the first to be reaped in Achaia, and they have laid themselves out to serve the saints. Well, I want you to put yourselves under people like that, under everyone who sets his hand to the work. . . . The churches of Asia salute you. Aquila and Prisca, with the church that meets in their house, salute you warmly in the Lord. All the brotherhood salutes you."

"As we have opportunity, let us do good to all men and in particular to the household of the faith."

"Thus you are strangers and foreigners no longer, you share the membership of the saints, you belong to God's own household, you are a building that rests on the apostles and prophets as its foundation, with Christ Jesus as the cornerstone; in him the whole structure is welded together and rises into a sacred temple in the Lord, and in him you are yourselves built into this to form a habitation for God in the Spirit."

"Paul a prisoner of Christ Jesus and brother Timotheus, to our beloved fellow-worker Philemon, to our sister Apphia, to our fellow-soldier Archippus, and to the church that meets in your house: grace and peace to you from God our Father and the Lord Jesus Christ."

The home was the original church, and though the word *ecclesia* has been enlarged beyond its original meaning, it still derives from the family hearth. Christian unity is a conformity of families, disciplined and directed by the gospel of a new life. Christianity is domestic, intimate, and personal; and wherever any home is loyal to the gospel of the new life, there is the church whose foundations rest upon the facts of the cross and the open tomb.

We have already returned to Corinth of the first century. Let us now go on a journey to Rome of that period. We are familiar with the sad story of Roman civilization and the reason why it fell. The hearth had been violated; the ancient dignity of consecrated love-relations had been insulted. Had we resided at Rome, with what eagerness should we have read the Ephesian letter when at last it found its way to the street on which we lived. We had accepted the facts of the gospel. Jesus had died and was now alive forevermore. Some of us had been living in Rome at the time of the crucifixion. Possibly a rumor of what had taken place in that far-away province of Judea had reached us a few months after the event. We were curious and wanted to know more about this glorious Man of Galilee who went about doing good and teaching a new way of living. Even then it appealed to us, though we were sceptical and wondered if the stories were not inventions.

But, at last, through the teaching of Peter or Paul or one of the other disciples, we had come under the banner of Jesus. How that act of surrender changed our point of view, tired of a reeking and corrupt society! As husbands and wives, we looked on one another in reverence and awe. We saw ourselves not as trees but as gods walking. We were now of the heavenly colony. Though we were not fully emancipated from the thraldom of the old world, we were pressing toward our inheritance along the path of a new discipline which, as we tried it, lifted our love for one another to heights of which we had never dreamed. Simplicity, tenderness, and understanding were now the marks of our regenerated life. We knew that we could not enter into our inheritance unless we consecrated wedded love. This knowledge made us eager to receive every bit of information which the inspired teachers so gladly communicated. How we would ponder over such words as these:

"Be strictly careful then about the life you lead; act like sensible men, not like thoughtless; make the very most of your time, for these are evil days."

Evil days? Yes. Rome was trembling to its foundations under the impact of a profligacy which filled the nights with the roar of drunken voices and with shrieks of laughter so tragic that we trembled at the sound of a mirth which could not cover the quivering despair of the revellers in the streets. At least we would make our home beautiful for God, a centre for the demonstration of the new life which He had given us in Jesus, the resurrected One.

So we should come to another portion of the letter with its tender admonition concerning the relationship of wives and husbands. Christ loved the home, the church,—*our* home. He gave himself up to consecrate that home by cleansing it in the bath of baptism into which we entered when we confessed our faith in him, rejecting the world which roared and shrieked outside. Our home must be his very own, standing before him in all its glory with never a spot or wrinkle or any such flaw, but consecrated and unblemished.

Then we should look up from this letter and vow a new allegiance to one another. For we knew that only by such allegiance could we make our home Christ's church. Then we should address ourselves to the problems of that home. One thing we could do: change our attitude to our slaves. They, like ourselves, were children of God, joint heirs with the Master in the new life. How eagerly we would seek to communicate that life to them! Perhaps it was one of those slaves who had brought us the knowledge of the gospel. The witness of a noble simplicity and devotion to the Master had so wrought upon us that the humble servant was now a royal ambassador of God. Perhaps, after reading this letter, we should find our way to the prison where Paul himself was now confined, though still allowed to speak through its iron gratings to those who sought a word with him. He, too, was a slave—the slave of Jesus, as he liked to call himself. And again we should hear him say in his own voice as he blessed us:

"Masters, act by your servants in the same way and stop threatening them; be sure that they and you have a Lord and Master in heaven, and there is no partiality about him."

We should lower our eyes at these words, remembering every act of injustice to those who were under our care; and in our heart we should cry to Jesus: "Great Servant, who so loved the world as to bear upon thy back its burdens and its sins, forgive our injustice to our servants. Teach us to be good masters, and help us to become a servant of servants."

The old problems of educating our family would also disappear. We should be related to our dear ones in the spirit of divine fellowship. All harshness of manner toward them would be softened into a tenderness that would make them feel the authority of the new life which we had found. We should discover that children are essentially spiritual and religious; that boys and girls are idealists, loving the beautiful. We should be beautiful in ourselves and give reality to their ideals by demonstrating them in the home.

Have we not lost something by divorcing the

church from the home? Many of us feel that we have. For that reason, we argue that Christianity is primarily a religion of lovers; that wherever love is noble, disciplined, and pure, the power of the Resurrection is manifested.

Of course, this interpretation is open to a question: "How does this bear upon the lives of the lonely? We do not all have the mystery of wedded love in our hearts. Many of us have never known that kind of love—will never know it. Where, then, can we find the church?"

Paul would answer at once by saying: "You have to live somewhere. Make your lonely room a household of fellowship. If you have found the new life, you will want to communicate it. Surely you have some friends who come to your lonely place. Exorcise that loneliness by little acts of gracious hospitality, for the Master has said, 'Where two or three have gathered together in my spirit, I am there among them.' "

The principle is sound and universal; no one of us is deprived of the right to utilize it in our lives. Open wide your arms to your world as your Master did and say, "Come unto me, all you who are weary and tired, and rest a while with me." Our life is crowded with glorious men and women who have turned their loneliness into such a fellowship of loving service that wherever they go, the church of God goes with them. They have become priests of the new communion of the spirit of the Master. Their hearts are his altar and their deeds its sacrament.

One of America's greatest poets has gathered these thoughts up in a beautiful poem of service. Anna Hempstead Branch is herself a servant of Christ, communicating the glory of the new life which she has found in Jesus. Her song of service is called "The Monk in the Kitchen":

> "One time in the cool of dawn
> Angels came and worked with me.
> The air was soft with many a wing.
> They laughed amid my solitude
> And cast bright looks on everything.
> Sweetly of me did they ask
> That they might do my common task.
> And all were beautiful—but one
> With garments whiter than the sun
> Had such a face
> Of deep, remembered grace,
> That when I saw I cried—'Thou art
> The great Blood-Brother of my heart.

Where have I seen thee?'—And he said,
'When we are dancing 'round God's throne,
How often thou art there.
Beauties from thy hands have flown
Like white doves wheeling in mid-air.
Nay—thy soul remembers not?
Work on, and cleanse thine iron pot.'"

PRAYER

O God, who hast made the families of men on earth to be guided and controlled by loving sacrifice, through the relationship of husbands, wives, children, and servants, we come to know Thee as the Father of us all. Grant that we, who have been called and elected to the discipleship of Jesus, may fulfill the obligations of our calling. May we always bear about in our bodies the marks of our discipleship. Forgive us when we fail, through idle words and careless deeds, to let the light that is in us shine among men.

Bless the love that we have for one another. Bless our homes, that we may be loyal to our ideals. When we are tempted to forsake them, look upon us and stir us to memory, as Peter was stirred when he denied Jesus. Pierce us with the gaze of divine love. Wound us with that love, until we return unto Thee. May Jesus, who manifested his divine Sonship at a wedding feast, be always visible in our homes, turning the water of our tears into the wine of the new life which we would drink with him at the table of his disciples.   Amen.

XIX

STARS IN A DARK WORLD
Philippians ii : 12–18

"Therefore, my beloved, as you have been obedient always and not simply when I was present, so, now that I am absent, work all the more strenuously at your salvation with reverence and trembling, for it is God who in his good-will enables you to will this and to achieve it. In all that you do, avoid grumbling and disputing, so as to be blameless and innocent, faultless children of God in a crooked and perverse generation where you shine like stars in a dark world; hold fast the word of life, so that I can be proud of you on the Day of Christ, because I have not run or worked for nothing. Even if my life-blood has to be poured as a libation on the sacred sacrifice of faith you are offering to God, I rejoice, I congratulate you all—and you in turn must rejoice and congratulate me."

THERE is no mistaking these words, written

by a man who had come out of danger and knew that every step of the way before him was marked by peril. He bore in his soul the wounds of many a fight. He would not have his friends misunderstand him: the possession of the new life in Jesus was no easy thing.

This he had learned from his Master, who had taught him to pray: "Lead us not into temptation." He understood that petition. To him it was a warning from one who had walked the steep ascent of heaven through peril, toil, and pain. Though many have expressed their distaste of that petition, or have tried to evade it by explaining it away, we are confronted by the fact that the path of initiation is perilous. Not that we are to be discouraged; Paul would never admit discouragement. He kept himself brave by forgetting what lay behind him, knowing that, as he dwelled upon the defeats of yesterday, it robbed him of power to make his conquests in to-day.

"You can win, but you must fight to win," he said over and over again to his followers. But it was a real fight:

"The weapons of my warfare are not weapons of

the flesh, but divinely strong to demolish fortresses—I demolish theories and any rampart thrown up to resist the knowledge of God, I take every project prisoner to make it obey Christ, I am prepared to court-martial anyone who remains insubordinate, once your submission is complete."

It is idle for us to think of attaining the power of the Resurrection without measuring the hardships that are in the road. We have all come through the period of explaining away damnation and punishment. We were driven to that because of the hard, literal doctrine of never-ending hellfire and of the wrath of God. We were wounded by this doctrine because it conflicted with the Master's teaching about the love of God. Knowing what love does and having somewhat of love in our hearts, we felt it an indignity to the love of God to describe Him as ever angry or vindictive. The doctrine of everlasting reprobation seemed to strike at the very roots of the gospel of the divine Master.

This was good thinking, but there was danger in it. Many of us are likely to forget that all high things are won as we seek them. Can we think of a hellfire hotter than that which a lover feels who remembers how he bartered love for selfishness? Can we think of any damnation more terrible than that of one who must admit to himself that he has been disloyal to a cause—a cause which, while he loved it, he betrayed because he loved himself more?

This plaint of the soul sounds through the praise of all the saints. Though Paul declared that he had forgotten what lay behind him, he occasionally remembered, as when he mourned: "I once believed it my duty indeed actively to oppose the name of Jesus the Nazarene." From his conversion, to the moment when he was led outside the Roman wall and bared his neck for the sword of the executioner, he never forgot the accusing eyes of the martyred Stephen. The nearer Paul got to Jesus, the more he regretted his past. As the beauty of the Resurrection dawned upon him, he shuddered at the memory of the deep abysses into which he might at any time have plunged.

In the struggle of our age to re-state its faith in sensible terms, we have lost the better part of that grim courage which made the religion of our fathers more vital and strengthening than ours would appear at times to be.

against the companions of light. The mystics have described these intelligences. Jesus was aware of them and once identified his earthly opponents with these intelligences when he said: "You belong to your father the devil, and you want to do what your father desires; he was a slayer of men from the very beginning, and he has no place in the truth because there is no truth in him: when he tells a lie, he is expressing his own nature, for he is a liar and the father of lies."

Was Jesus ignorant of the universe? Was he merely an inspired peasant, revealing the subtle beauties of a literary righteousness incorporated in a book called the Old Testament—a righteousness which he made personal by the purity of his life and the heroism of his death? "No," answers Paul; and "No," answer all who believe with him that Jesus is the first-born of many brethren.

Christianity is a spiritual brotherhood, a communion of saints, or, as Paul described it, a heavenly colony. We who have accepted Jesus as Master belong to that colony and are one with all the sons of light. We must be loyal to their cause. How can we be loyal if we ignore what the Master declared in his teaching concerning the powers of light and the powers of darkness? There have been, from the beginning of time as it measures the life of man on this planet, diabolical souls who have always resisted the sons of God. These souls are remembered in the stories of the dreadful cruelties of ancient kings who punctured the eyes of their victims and poured lead into their nostrils, impaled children on stakes, laughing at their shrieks of agony. Nero, driving a chariot around his garden under the flares of the burning bodies of Christian saints, mediæval lords with their torture chambers, sadistic priests who revelled in the cruelties of the Inquisition, force us to realize that Jesus and Paul were not rhetorical when they spoke of the devil and all his angels.

Our warfare is indeed a real one, a warfare with powers, with angelic rulers, authorities, potentates of the dark present, spiritual forces of evil in the heavenly sphere. He who would attain the power of the Resurrection must listen to Paul, who urged the disciples of his day to be strong in the Lord and the strength of his might, to put on God's armor so as to be able to stand against the stratagems of the devil. Obedience to that injunction is imperative. We cannot trifle with the forces of evil. We must awake to righteousness and sin not. We must put on all the armor of God, clothing ourselves with the resurrection body. Whatever strikes against the reality of that body is a peril to the soul which has entered the path of discipleship.

We know the outer darkness of the damned. That world is about us. It is the place where the gossips and the back-biters dwell. To that world belong murderers and thieves, people of horrible unnatural habits and practices. Out of that world come wars, cruelties, wrongs. It is a real world, a terrible world, a world in which once we lived and which, by the grace of Jesus and the love of God and the fellowship of the Spirit, we have renounced. That world is not confined to our planet. Its boundaries extend beyond our present experience of time and space.

As man has two bodies, so he lives in two worlds at the same time—the world of matter and the world of spirit. Death does not launch us into a place of utter peace. God is not yet all in all. The fight is still toward. Nor can God be all in all until His sons have surrendered to Him. Jesus fully surrendered: "Therefore God raised him high and conferred on him a Name above all names." By that surrender, Jesus changed the balance of the fight in favor of God, against the dark powers. There is a deep implication of this truth in one of Jesus' last words on the cross: "It is finished." Be on the side of the sons of light and wage your warfare under the banner of the cross.

PRAYER

Grant to us, Eternal Father, the understanding of the perils that lie in the way of discipleship. Though we would not consult our fears, we would remember that we have before us a hard fight to lay hold on that life which is ours for the winning. We who ask Thee not to lead us into temptation recognize that there are dangers always lurking behind the boulders and in the forests, on the deserts and among the mountains of the upward trail. He who taught us to ask Thee not to lead us into temptation was teaching us not to tempt Thee by ignoring the path and its perils.

We would put on the whole armor of our divine sonship, that we may be able to help in the winning of that warfare of righteousness in which Thy sons have been engaged from the beginning. Keep us from trifling, from deserting, from forgetting. When we are wounded in the conflict, heal us by the anointing of that grace of Jesus which heals all hurts and restores us again to the work of a soldier of the cross. This we ask in his name.   Amen.

XX

VISIBLE AND INVISIBLE WORLDS

II Corinthians xii : 2–10

"I know a man in Christ who fourteen years ago was caught up to the third heaven. In the body or out of the body? That I do not know: God knows. I simply know that in the body or out of the body (God knows which) this man was caught up to paradise and heard sacred secrets which no human lips can repeat. Of an experience like that I am prepared to boast, but not of myself personally—not except as regards my weaknesses. (If I did care to boast of other things, I would be no 'fool,' for I would have a true tale to tell; however, I abstain from that—I want no one to take me for more than he can see in me or make out from me.) My wealth of visions might have puffed me up, so I was given a thorn in the flesh, an angel of Satan to rack me and keep me from being puffed up; three times over I prayed the Lord to make it leave me, but he told me, 'It is enough

for you to have my grace: it is in weakness that [my] power is fully felt.' So I am proud to boast of all my weakness, and thus to have the power of Christ resting on my life. It makes me satisfied, for Christ's sake, with weakness, insults, trouble, persecution, and calamity; for I am strong just when I am weak."

As man has two bodies, so he lives in two worlds at the same time. By the first body he lives in the world of matter. By the second body he lives in the world of spirit. The world of spirit interpenetrates the world of matter, which, in turn, blends into the world of spirit. "Heaven lies about us in our infancy," and it surrounds us to the end of our earthly life. So we live in heaven or hell as we occupy the body of spirit or of matter. "The interests of the flesh meant death, the interests of the Spirit meant life and peace."

Science has opened up for the Christian new vistas of the interpenetration of the worlds of matter and spirit, which indicate that our rational processes do not necessarily contradict our spiritual experiences. Christianity is in-

pains to warn us against dark rulers in heavenly places.

What does Paul mean by heavenly places? In answering this question, we admit his intellectual limitations. He did not know anything about the island theory of the universe. He was as ignorant of modern physics as Aristotle was. But he had had an experience with astral or etheric matter, which he described when he wrote:

"I know a man in Christ who fourteen years ago was caught up to the third heaven. In the body or out of the body? That I do not know: God knows. I simply know that in the body or out of the body this man was caught up to paradise and heard sacred secrets which no human lips can repeat."

There is a world beyond the atom and the electron, the ultra-violet ray and the bubbling muted note of the hermit thrush. The mystics know of

"The light that never was, on sea or land;
The consecration, and the Poet's dream."

This world has two aspects, the one positive, the other negative. The first is heaven, the second, hell. But between these poles of spiritual reality there is an intermediate state. This state is the abode of discarnate souls, who have laid aside their bodies as they moved through the gate of death. The blessed dead are they who, in departing, find themselves in bodies which are adapted to their new environment—spiritual bodies, bodies which they had before their departure from the visible world, trained and prepared by obedience to the discipline of the risen Christ.

For souls who are unprepared by that discipline, death is a disaster, fraught with unspeakable agonies. Jesus did not lightly speak of those who move in an outer darkness. It is a reality to be faced. So Paul urged men to work out their own salvation in fear and trembling. Dante's description of the Inferno, however it was weighted with the popular symbology of his time, was true to the teaching of Jesus and of Paul. The damned are prisoners of dark authorities, who, by the exercise of a deliberate will toward evil, have gained control over that world of matter which lies beyond the atom.

One of the most significant preachers of our

down all other rulers, all other authorities and powers. For he must reign until all his foes are put under his feet. (Death is the last foe to be put down.) For God has put everything under his feet. When it is said that everything has been put under him, plainly that excludes Him who put everything under him; and when everything is put under him, then the Son himself will be put under Him who put everything under him, so that God may be everything to everyone."

Can we understand these words, which have baffled the centuries? It is our belief that hell is impermanent; that it lasts only as long as souls determine it by their disobedience. Though the effects of this disobedience involve the soul in disasters which surpass man's power to describe, God will have His way with us all. What is that way? Jesus is the answer. The cross is the way of God. He Himself is involved in man's disobedience. That disobedience delays Him. Sin is highway robbery, forcing God to stand that it may rob Him of His goods. Think of the goods of God—His blessings, the riches which He would bestow on us and which we steal from Him. We cannot enjoy the riches of God that way. We enjoy them by inheritance, not by robbery. To inherit the riches of God, we must enter into His life and learn how to work with Him. Then we shall have His goods.

How can a man work with God? Jesus answers: "My food is to do the will of him who sent me, and to accomplish his work. . . . The Son of man has come to seek and save the lost." Our salvation makes us saviours!

"Treat one another with the same spirit as you experience in Christ Jesus," wrote Paul to the Philippians. This explains his passion of preaching, his going forth to the ends of the earth to rescue the lost. Not only here but beyond this world, the hosts of light are engaged in the rescue of the hosts of darkness—a strange battle, in which one side fights to save and the other to destroy. We who know the redeeming power of love can have no uncertainty about the ultimate victory of God. However delayed that victory, the end will come when He shall be all in all.

We are aware that we are open to a charge of inconsistency in this interpretation of the gospel of universal salvation. Some will say: "If you teach this, sinners will continue in their disobedience, enjoying themselves while they are under the dominion of the flesh, faintly hoping that somehow, in the end, all will be well." But that is not what we teach. We have described the terrible disaster of disobedience. But how can we hearten ourselves to enter into alliance with the host of salvation unless we believe that, however hard the fight, the victory will be ours? This should add zeal to the saviours of the world, patience to those who, on the outposts, are engaged in what seems to be a losing battle. "Courage!" says the Master; "I have overcome the world of disobedient matter. I will draw all men unto me."

PRAYER

Eternal Love, who art ever new, meeting us in all the changes of our mortal and spiritual life, to Thee we bow in adoration of Thy holiness. Only as we know Thee are we able to measure that word. Without that holiness there is no salvation. We are saved as we are purified, for only the pure in heart know Thee. Guide us as Thou didst guide our fathers, until Thou art manifested in us. Thy holiness is our heaven. It is our prize. We have found it in Jesus and, having found it, are hungry and thirsty for it.

We thank Thee for him who had all Thy holiness in his manhood, teaching us by his life how to gain this prize of our high calling. Thou hast called us to be holy. By the challenge of his holiness may we wrestle, fight, and, casting all the powers of darkness down, win the well-fought day. Amen.

XXI

GOD'S ARMOR

Ephesians vi : 10–20

"Be strong in the Lord and in the strength of his might; put on God's armour so as to be able to stand against the stratagems of the devil. For we have to struggle, not with blood and flesh but with the angelic Rulers, the angelic Authorities, the potentates of the dark present, the spirit-forces of evil in the heavenly sphere. So take God's armour, that you may be able to make a stand upon the evil day and hold your ground by overcoming all the foe. Hold your ground, tighten the belt of truth about your loins, wear integrity as your coat of mail, and have your feet shod with the stability of the gospel of peace; above all, take faith as your shield, to enable you to quench all the fire-tipped darts flung by the evil one, put on salvation as your helmet, and take the Spirit as your sword (that is, the word of God), praying at all times in the Spirit with all manner of

prayer and entreaty—be alive to that, attend to it unceasingly, interceding on behalf of all the saints and on my behalf also, that I may be allowed to speak and open my lips in order to expound fully and freely that open secret of the gospel for the sake of which I am in custody as its envoy. Pray that I may have freedom to declare it as I should."

WHAT simplicity and tenderness mark the completion of the Ephesian letter—a letter of heights and depths: heights of an awful glory through which we dimly behold the face of our Father God in the face of our Brother Jesus; depths of an indescribable darkness into which that glory plunges like a sword, the sword of the cross! The heights are for man to gain; the depths are for him to leave. Between those heights and those depths what meadow-lands, what open roads, what songs of companionship, what interchange of spiritual adventure, are discovered!

Paul has prepared us for this moment in his survey of the height, the depth, the length, and the breadth of the full experience of the sons

HIS GLORIOUS BODY

of God in their quest for the holiness of their Infinite Father. It is a moment of simplicity and tenderness, as of a comrade who does not withdraw himself from us in this struggle to attain, but takes us into his confidence, cheering us on by the nobility of words that tell us to put on all of God's armor. There is an armor of God. God is a warrior, who calls us into battle. That battle has been described for us in the All Saints' Day hymn:

> "The Son of God goes forth to war,
> A kingly crown to gain;
> His blood-red banner streams afar:
> Who follows in His train?"

We are to be strong in the Lord and in the strength of His might. The strength of that might is acquired as we wear His armor. We are face to face with angelic rulers, authorities, potentates in the dark present, spirit-forces of evil in the heavenly sphere.

First, we are to hold our ground; however small, it is part of the conquered area of God. We may look upon ourselves with contempt, saying, "How puny we are; how insignificant is our contribution to the campaign of God

GOD'S ARMOR

against the spirit-forces of evil. Who are we to engage in this struggle, that covers the history of man's life on this planet?" Beyond the caveman, down to our moment, God's warfare has continued and will continue until He is victorious. What ground have we gained? However small, it is important. Remember the hour when, like the boy Samuel, you called across the Infinite to the holiness of God, saying, "Speak, thy servant is listening." That is your ground—and how you have widened it! Be fair with yourself; have the courage to say with Paul, "By God's grace I am what I am." We weaken ourselves if we belittle what we have thus far gained for God. Value the treasure which lies hidden somewhere in the field of experience, and which will be found and possessed as we wrestle, fight, and pray.

There is a lovely tradition that seeks to explain Paul's metaphor of the armor of God. He was living at Rome, under the custody of a soldier, sharing the same room with him. Every morning Paul used to watch the soldier as he put on the armor of Cæsar, and noticed how he tied a rope about his loose-fitting tunic before putting on the coat of mail. After that came the sandals, the shield, the helmet, and finally the stout cross-hilted sword, worn on the left thigh.

Let us follow the metaphor through, and begin with the girdle of truth—the truth that now are we the sons of God. We must wear that truth about our soul. Do not wear it loosely; wear it as a discipline until our full selfhood responds to its pressure. The truth of our divine sonship is limiting, in the sense of its spiritual restrictions. We know what these restrictions are; Paul has described them for us:

"But I possess this treasure in a frail vessel of earth, to show that the transcending power belongs to God, not to myself; on every side I am harried but not hemmed in, perplexed but not despairing, persecuted but not abandoned, struck down but not destroyed."

We must make no compromise with the world about the truth of our divinity. We must wear it tightly until it hurts, in the discipline of self-control. We must wear it about our thoughts, our words, and our deeds, until we are freed from the entanglements of the flesh by the imprison-

GOD'S ARMOR

ing red girdle of the truth that now are we God's sons.

After that comes the breastplate of God's character. The breastplate is worn above the heart. The heart knows God, wants Him; for the heart describes love, without which no one can see God. Our inmost craving for God's character follows the girdle of the truth of our potential divinity. God's character is His divinity. Divinity is something in God that can be communicated; something in us that wants what God seeks to give. Once we wear that breastplate of God's character, we walk at ease, like the psalmist who wrote:

"Happy the man who stays by the Most High in shelter,
who lives under the shadow of Almighty God,
who calls the Eternal 'My refuge and my fortress,
my God in whom I trust'!"

God needs our consecrated manhood and womanhood. He has called us through the centuries into His battle. We must be girded with truth and breasted with righteousness. This righteousness describes the soul in its integrity. An integer is a number that is complete in itself,

HIS GLORIOUS BODY

And integrity describes our character with nothing left out—the whole man completed and united in one communion and fellowship of body, mind, and spirit, glorious with the character of God as it is revealed in Jesus.

Next we must put on the sandals of the stability of a peaceful gospel. Have we not done that in this age? The saints of the past did not wear those sandals as we are wearing them. It was left to us to complete the armor of God with the sandals of peace. We look with understanding upon the various religious cults of our world, for ours is the age of international and inter-ecclesiastical fellowship. We are not discouraged by our difficulties. We do not expect to establish the kingdom of God in a moment. The experience of the first century has taught us to await with patience the coming of our Lord. But we believe that he wants us to do all we can to open wide the bronze gates of tradition which shut him out, that he may enter into this world in the fulness of his glory.

Was Paul thinking of Pheidippides, who ran from Marathon to Athens with the news of victory? Like him we would run, crying, "Glory

GOD'S ARMOR

to God in the highest, and on earth peace to men of God's will!" Jesus wears those sandals; through him God comes down the ages to us with a word of good news. If we would share with Paul the power of the Resurrection, we must not neglect the sandals of reconciliation. A gospel that is not radiant with the spirit of peace is a mutilated gospel. There can be no catholicity without that message of peace. As we press forward with the good news of the kingdom of God, we must have the spirit of Pheidippides, whose heart was broken by the strain of his breathless running as a messenger of peace. Who shall hold us back with old wives' tales and counsels of fearful spirits? "Let no one hold you back," Paul would say; "forget what lies behind. Do not look over your shoulder as you run, but press toward the mark with the sandals of a peaceful gospel."

Now comes the shield of faith. We like that definition of faith. Paul had much to say about faith, but he never thought of it as a blind or obedient acquiescence to verbal authorities. His faith was a shield—part of the armor of a good soldier, who had to be as dextrous with

HIS GLORIOUS BODY

his shield as he was with his sword. The two were used together, the one for defense, the other for attack. Our faith must be defensive. It can only be that as we use it. When David was invited to wear the shield of Saul, he threw it aside because he had not proved it. What an honor to wear the shield of a warrior like Saul; and yet David refused it. When a man is engaged in fighting, he is not concerned with honors. What are honors or dignities in a life-and-death struggle with one's foes?

A shield has use only as one has tried it. Our faith is our experience with the power of the Resurrection. Let us not be tempted, in the battle for God, to wear anything which we have not proved by experience. That is what Paul would say to us about our modern religious difficulties. He was never a conformist, never orthodox in the sense of the word as we have come to use it. He would say: "Your faith is what you have proved. How can you prove anything until you have dared to try it? Try the thoughts of your heart by your words and your deeds. Work out your own scheme of salvation in spite of your fears and your tremblings. Stand in your own right when you see the white anger on the faces of men who oppose you because of your independence of thought and life."

Put on salvation as *your* helmet. It must be *your* helmet. You have a right to say, "I am saved!" For you are saved, if you have met Jesus. However uncertain you may be of the way that lies before you, walk therein without fear. How can we be fearful when the way is marked with the footprints of the Master?

The glorious fact of the gospel is that it is a helmet of salvation. Jesus has proved our deathlessness. This knowledge is our helmet. We must wear it with joy and with courage as we go on our way through the doubts of our world. Christianity has always needed convinced disciples. It needs them at this hour, with all these voices proclaiming the supremacy of death. Modern intellectualism has insulted the human soul by dividing it into parts and throwing it away. We are souls—sons of the living God. When we know that we are sons of God, we are saved—saved from cowardice, from uncertainty, from despair. What a glorious thing it is to put on the helmet of our salvation!

The helmet covers the head as the breastplate covers the heart. The heart knows the nature of God's character, hungers and thirsts for it. The head enthrones our thought. Jesus said that salvation is thought: "This is eternal life, that they know thee, the only real God." Was it John who added: "And him whom thou hast sent, even Jesus Christ"? We doubt if Jesus said it, but we believe that whoever added that to the story of the prayer in the Upper Room knew his business, and we are one with him in saying that the knowledge of God is incomplete if we leave out Jesus Christ, whom God sent to us with the good news of the gospel of peace. Knowing God through Jesus is a protection against all doubt concerning the nature and the destiny of man. Our thoughts, under the helmet of salvation, are protected against all the blows of a blind intellectualism which derides the integrity of the soul and laughs at our faith in the power of the Resurrection.

Read what you will. Analyze and digest all the writings of this generation. The helmet of our salvation will protect us against agnosticism or atheism, for as our heart sings, our head will proclaim with Paul, "Christ did rise from the dead, he was the first to be reaped of those who sleep in death."

What is the sword of the Spirit? Paul tells us "the word of God," and if we ask about the word of God, the Beloved Disciple will reply in his prologue to the Fourth Gospel:

> "The Logos existed in the very beginning,
> the Logos was with God,
> the Logos was divine.
> He was with God in the very beginning:
> through him all existence came into being,
> no existence came into being apart from him.
> In him life lay,
> and this life was the Light for men:
> amid the darkness the Light shone,
> but the darkness did not master it. . . .
> He entered the world—
> the world which existed through him—
> and yet the world did not recognize him;
> he came to what was his own, yet his own folk did
>   not welcome him.

"On those who have accepted him, however, he has conferred the right of being children of God, that is, on those who believe in his Name, who owe this birth of theirs to God, not to human blood, nor to any impulse of the flesh or of man. The Logos became flesh and tarried among us; we have seen his glory— glory such as an only son enjoys from his father— seen it to be full of grace and reality."

HIS GLORIOUS BODY

Jesus is the word of God. We do not doubt that. No soldier doubts his sword. He has proved it, as he has proved his shield. However we may be separated in our interpretations of creeds and theologies, we are united in the belief that Jesus is the word of God. What word? God's message to us concerning ourselves. We are His sons. This knowledge is our sword. Draw the sword of the knowledge of your divine sonship and enter into the battle of God against the dark rulers of the world—men who repudiate their divinity and ours, and who use every device of enthroned authorities to scatter our forces and make us prisoners of despair.

A shield is a weapon of defense; a sword, of attack. We belong to the church militant, and though the weapons of our warfare are spiritual, not carnal, there is a warfare. How can we fight the massed battalions of materialism unless we are rooted and grounded in the knowledge of Jesus? We must make no apology for him. We know him and this knowledge is our sword. The aggressive life of Christianity is a life of sublime service. The sublimity of that service is the measure of our exultant faith in the ulti-

GOD'S ARMOR

mate salvation of the human race. The certainty of that salvation must direct our sword-strokes against whatever damns humanity. Saviourhood is demanded of us by him who said, "Go into all the world and teach the nations." What have we to teach the nations? This: We are all brothers and sons of one Father. Yes, we must put on the whole armor of God: the girdle of truth, the breastplate of integrity, the shield of faith, the sandals of peace, the helmet of salvation, and the sword of the word.

PRAYER

O Lamb of God, lifted on a cross to challenge our souls, lead us by the way of thy great giving—the way that goes through the bitterness of betrayal and the loneliness of desertion—to the unity of thy soul with God. Show us every step of that way; however it winds and turns through the briars and the thorns, may we always behold the imprint of thy feet.

Help us to put on the whole armor of God, our loins girt about with truth, that we may know the freedom that is found as we accept its binding circumference. May we wear the

HIS GLORIOUS BODY

breastplate of God's character as thou didst wear it. Dear Master, our feet cannot stay on the path without thy sandals, nor can our heads be proud and brave without the helmet of thy salvation. Bless us as we kiss the cross of the swordhilt of thy word, so that we may fight the good fight of faith and lay hold on eternal life. Amen.

XXII

OUR BELOVED BROTHER

Ephesians vi : 21–24

"Our beloved brother Tychicus, a faithful minister in the Lord, will give you all information about me, so that you may know how I am; that is why I am sending him to you, to let you know how I am and to encourage your hearts.

"Peace and love with faith be to the brothers from God the Father and the Lord Jesus Christ. Grace be with all who have an undying love for our Lord Jesus Christ."

WE have come a long way together. We began with the two experiences fundamental to Christian faith—the cross of a redeeming Saviour and the victorious Resurrection of an all-including Christ. These facts account for Christianity through the years. As men and women have received and applied them, their lives have been inspired and beautiful. The Church is a witness to the power of these facts.

Paul's letters were written out of an experience which changed his life. Deny the experience and we deny the letters. Written under duress of busy days of a unique ministry, they witness to the validity of the experience itself. Otherwise Paul is guilty of a fiction which would make him the greatest impostor this planet has known. Can we think that of one who encompassed his world for the truth of the gospel?

From our study of these letters, we have found many things, and among them these: Jesus died that we might live. He announced himself as one who came to confer upon all men the consciousness of the more abundant life of the children of God. Jesus had this life in himself. He revealed it among men in the days of his flesh. The Fourth Gospel ends with an intimation of the scope of the historic life of Jesus from the cradle to the cross: "Now there is much else that Jesus did—so much, that if it were written down in detail, I do not suppose the world itself could hold the written records."

At the end of the first century, as men looked back over the brief years of the Master's life, they were amazed at its fulness. This fulness justified them in believing that through Jesus, God and men had entered into a new way of living. He had "put down death and brought life and immortality to light by the gospel." What is the gospel? Good news, news about God given to men for the first time. The disciples had begun with news about God; they were Hebrews, living in a country which had given to the world a Book about God. But this was not the particular news which Paul and his brother disciples gave to the first century.

As that century was closing, some one wrote a letter to the Hebrews. He began by saying:

"Many were the forms and fashions in which God spoke of old to our fathers by the prophets, but in these days at the end he has spoken to us by a Son —a Son whom he appointed heir of the universe, as it was by him that he created the world. He, reflecting God's bright glory and stamped with God's own character, sustains the universe with his word of power; when he had secured our purification from sins, he sat down at the right hand of the Majesty on high."

This helps us to distinguish between the old and the new information about God as the disciples themselves regarded it. Though they looked with reverence upon the scriptures, believing that they witnessed to the truth of the gospel, they did not confound that gospel with the news of God which the Old Testament had carried to them and their fathers through the ages. The gospel is not to be identified with the Old Testament. It is a new thing, and wherever Christianity has confused this gospel with the Old Testament, it has mutilated or destroyed the message as it came from those whose joy was founded on the fact that they had seen, heard, and touched Jesus.

The life of Jesus is as potent now as it was in the first century. His name is on every tongue. Men speak of him with reverence, however they may differ among themselves in the conclusions which they are bound to draw as they obey his word, "Handle me and see." It is as we handle him and see that we come at last to understand the grandeur of Paul's letters and their bearing upon our present life. The life of Jesus represents the highest altitude of humanity. We can describe Socrates, Plato, Aristotle; we can fit Dante and Shakespeare into our human categories. But Jesus always

OUR BELOVED BROTHER

transcends our thoughts and our words. How volatile the spirit of Jesus is, and how we are humbled whenever we try to measure him, even as we are exalted in our efforts!

The gospel derives from an historic life which opened our era. Whether we accept him or no, we divide time by the event of the birth of a child whom his mother named Jesus. Who was Jesus? Our answer determines our relationship with him. But whatever that relationship is, it bears upon our destiny. Like Herod, we may insult him by demanding signs and wonders. Like Mary and her sons, we may wound him by failing to understand his passion for God. Like the disciples themselves, we may betray, deny, desert him. Or, like the thief on the cross, out of our humiliation we may declare him "the holiest among the mighty."

But whatever we think, say, or do, Jesus stands central to all humanity. Our age is aware of that, and of writing many books concerning him there seems to be no end. Whether we consult the four Gospels, the letters of Paul, the Epistle to the Hebrews, or the letters attributed to those who knew him when he was on earth,

HIS GLORIOUS BODY

we feel that Jesus is the most certain event in the history of humanity. He is the keystone of the arch of the ages. Without that stone the arch would collapse. The cross and the open tomb are inevitable to those who would find release from the despair of men who say in their heart, "There is no God." When we know Jesus as the disciples knew him, we must say, "There is God, for He was in Christ, reconciling the world unto Himself."

We do not attempt to offer any answer to the question, "Who was Jesus?" for we believe that this can only be answered as we receive him. The faith of Christianity is broad enough to include all relationships with our blessed Master. But we are one in hailing Jesus as the world's Redeemer. How has he redeemed us? Paul answers:

"First and foremost, I passed on to you what I had myself received, namely, that Christ died for our sins as the scriptures had said, that he was buried, that he rose on the third day as the scriptures had said, and that he was seen by Cephas, then by the twelve; after that, he was seen by over five hundred brothers all at once, the majority of whom survive to this day, though some have died; after that, he was seen by James, then by all the apostles, and finally he was seen by myself, by this so-called 'abortion' of an apostle."

To us who believe with Paul that Jesus has opened for us the way of a new life in God, this sentence comes as a challenge:

"Our beloved brother Tychicus, a faithful minister in the Lord, will give you all information about me, so that you may know how I am; that is why I am sending him to you, to let you know how I am and to encourage your hearts."

Our beloved brother Tychicus! Thank God for him. He is always in our midst, helping us to understand Paul and his message. Tychicus is the practical disciple. He does not pretend to the genius of Paul, who stands by himself and whom Tychicus is always eager to honor by the fidelity of his ministry of the cross and the open tomb. Every disciple must have in himself the witness of the cross and the Resurrection. Wherever we meet a man or a woman who has this witness, we find Tychicus.

He is, above all things, a man of prayer. Prayer is living close to God. The Old Testament has its foundation in men like Enoch, Abraham, Moses, and the prophets. The New

Testament is the story of One who surpassed these men in living close to God. This man was Jesus, and through him we understand what happens when we live like that. What happens? A new way of living. Death disappears as we live close to God; for how can any one fear death whose life is centred in God?

Jesus is supreme because he has demonstrated that there is something in man which never dies —the soul. When we deny the soul, we deny God. But when we discover that we are souls, we begin to live as Jesus lived. To be Tychicus, we must be men and women of prayer. We are not unmindful of some of the traditional forms of prayer; books of meditation, liturgies of the soul's approach to the Infinite, are useful and not to be decried. But these at best are introductions to the life of prayer. Prayer begins that moment when we are able to say with Jesus, "I and my Father are one," which means: "I am now living close to God, as a son with his father."

Begin with the truth upon which all the letters of Paul bear: God's soul witnesses with our soul that we are His sons. Why should it be thought a difficult thing that God should raise from death a son like Jesus? Has He not already raised us from death? In us dwells God's fulness. True, we have not measured it, nor have we yet power to demonstrate it. But we know that this power is already in us.

Like Tychicus, who obeyed his master, let us go forth with the assuring words: "All is well with our brother Paul." God has kept faith with him. Somewhere in the house not made with hands, Paul walks with his Master. His power is not waning.

This Tychicus knows and gladly shares with the world. He has no uncertainty about Paul's information; he has tested the cross and the open tomb. Tychicus is in the church, preaching from the pulpits. His words are glorious with the song of endless life. Without that song preaching is not valid. Tychicus is in the pews. Sometimes he preaches with greater power there than in the pulpit, for his life of courage and high consecration to service is a gospel of the cross and the Resurrection. Tychicus comes out of jails to the open spaces of the world. He has found a freedom which no prison can confine.

HIS GLORIOUS BODY

The world is ready for him, and as he goes, the song celestial increases with the multitude of ransomed souls who have heard the last trumpet and have been changed by its sound. That sound is a blast of victory, telling of a battle already won, though perils are still before those who have consecrated themselves to the warfare against the dark powers of death.

Rejoice and be glad that we have been summoned into the conflict which ends on such a victory that even the world is lost as we count its gains and discover that the death and the Resurrection of Jesus include all the universes of God. Our Master is on his way, and we are following in his train. It is the way of victory.

PRAYER

Master, teach us to pray. Give us the secret that imparts to those who possess it the power of living close to God. Thou art His great Son, but we are thy brothers and would follow thee whithersoever thou leadest us. How can we pray unless we follow thee? Along the ways of life we trace thy footsteps and, as we find and follow them, we draw near to God.

OUR BELOVED BROTHER

Thou art God, for in thee dwells His fulness. By living close to the Father thy manhood became divine. We believe that we, too, are heirs of that divinity, joint heirs with thee, if we submit to the disciplines which thou hast proved and demonstrated as ordeals of initiation into the life of Him from whom we derive our being.

We would share with thee the communion of saints, that with them we may inherit eternal life. Help us as we go upon our way, that we may not turn aside from the path which thou hast blessed with thy feet and made lovely with memories of thy going.   Amen.

252 N89H

BROOKLYN PUBLIC LIBRARY

This Book may be kept 14 days from the last date stamped below.
A fine of 2 CENTS will be charged for each day the Book is kept beyond that time.

4 Ag '30 Z	9 MY '31	
21 AG '30 W		
18 Se '30 V		
7 Oc '30 V	30 Ja '32	
Oc '30	2 Nov '31 N	
10 Oc '30	4 No '32 V	
5 No '30	27 Fe '33	
	10 Se '33 S	
8 No '30	20 Oc '33	
11 De '30		
31 Ja '31	7 Oc '33 S	
	18 No '33	
4 Fe '31		
16 Fe '31		
20 Fe '31		
9 Mr '31		
2 Apr '31		
17 JL '31		

Form Ds.